AN ACCESSIBLE WII

LIFE AT STANAGE
AND THE NORTH LEES ESTATE

Edited by Jenny Edgar,
Literature Development Officer,
Derbyshire County Council with the
Editorial Group of the Stanage Book Project

First published 2003 by
Derbyshire County Council
and the Peak District National Park Authority

ISBN 0 903463 73 3

©2003 Derbyshire County Council/Peak District National Park Authority

Design. Typesetting & production by Dick Richardson
Country Books, Courtyard Cottage, Little Longstone, Bakewell, Derbyshire DE45 1NN

Printed and bound in England by MPS, Wotton-under-Edge, Gloucestershire

CONTENTS

The Peak District Interpretation Project - Telling the Peak District Story

This book is one of many activities supported by the Peak District Interpretation Project.

The Project is a partnership working to 'Tell the Peak District Story' through a range of diverse and stimulating interpretive activities across the Peak District. The Project works over the geographical area of the Peak District rather than just within the National Park.

We are managed and funded by a partnership that is comprised of The Peak District National Park Authority, Derbyshire County Council, Derbyshire Dales District Council, High Peak Borough Council, Severn Trent Water, United Utilities and The National Trust. Additional funding has come from the European Union Economic Regional Development Fund.

Our aim is to promote understanding of the special qualities of the Peak District through the development of high quality interpretation. Our emphasis is on working in partnership with a very wide range of groups, organisations and individuals. We can provide help and advice to anyone looking to develop interpretation in the Peak District. The Project team is based at the National Park Study Centre, Losehill Hall, Castleton, Hope Valley S33 8WB and can be contacted either on 01433 620373 or email interpretation@peakdistrict-npa.gov.uk

Gavin Bell
Interpretation Project Officer

ACKNOWLEDGEMENTS

The Editorial Group would like to thank Derbyshire County Council, the Peak District National Park Authority and the Peak District Interpretation Project with assistance from the European Union Economic Regional Development Fund.

Thanks go to Nick Smith, Robert Helliwell, Mr Middleton, David Wright, the Peak District National Park Authority Ray Manley and members of the Prigent and Ollerenshaw families for the use of their photographs.

Thanks also to everyone who was interviewed for the book for their enthusiasm and commitment. Whilst it was not possible to include every story that was taped, copies of all interviews, with the original transcripts, will be held in the Local Studies Library at Matlock and at the Peak District National Park Authority at Losehill Hall, Castleton and will be available to the public.

CONTRIBUTORS:

Dianna Ackerman
Tom Armitage
Mary Bailey
Joe Bawden
Steve Bolton
Irene and John Bunting
Janice Burley
Matthew Croney
Marion Dale
Lois Edge
Lynn Ellis
Ted Ellerton
Bill Enningham
Leah Fleetwood
Nellie Frost
Mark Goodwin
Bill Gordon
Robert Helliwell
Mary Heyes
Jean Hodgkinson
Betty Horner
Terry Howard
Gordon Stainforth
Sheila Humphreys
Rick Jillings
Trevor Lawton
Betty Lloyd

Jane and John Marsden
Mary Marshall
Jean Monks
Arthur Ollerenshaw
Eric Ollerenshaw
Jabez Ollerenshaw
Stuart Ollerenshaw
Pat Peters
Ray Platts
Ron Priestley
Muriel Prigent
Freda Raphael
Flo Richardson
Eileen Robinson
Neil Roden
Margaret Sanderson
Margaret and Les Seaman
David Sissons
Patricia Smith
Evelyn Spink
James Thacker
Sheila Thompson
Madge and Ron Townsend
Roger Watson

FOREWORD

Set in the spectacular scenery of the Peak District National Park, Stanage Edge, just north of Hathersage, dominates the sky line. From north to south it measures approximately 5 kilometres and its stunning views and air of wilderness attracts people from all walks of life and with interests in different forms of leisure activity.

There are those who take their walking seriously as well as families out for a Sunday afternoon stroll. Climbers see it as a mecca, some even moving to the area to be near this famous climbing ground. They are inspired and challenged by climbs with the most wonderful names: Christmas Crack, The Unconquerable, The Flying Buttress and The Tippler, to name just a few. Para-gliders, hang-gliders and boulderers have joined the crowds of people who make their way to Stanage at all times of the year.

For some the literary connections with Charlotte Bronte, and her enduring novel, 'Jane Eyre', pulls them to North Lees Hall, that has stood for hundreds of years under Stanage Edge. There they walk in the footsteps of the novelist and see the area through her eyes.

Artists return year after year to try to capture on canvas or film the grandeur of the many faces of the area.

There is a natural attraction for bird-watchers and an abundance of flora and fauna offer both professional and 'week-end' enthusiasts the opportunity to enjoy and catalogue plants and animals that have inhabited Derbyshire for centuries.

Add to this the legends of Robin Hood, the champion of the poor, who is reputed to have hidden out in what is known as Robin Hood's Cave, the stories of Roman soldiers walking over The Edge and the industrial history of the salt roads and the millstone industry and it begins to be clear why this area draws people back again and again.

Stanage and North Lees Estate are surrounded by villages and hamlets, each of which has its own particular identity. Hathersage, its name said to be derived from 'Heather's Edge', a reference to the beautiful purple summer landscape, is the biggest settlement in the area. Bamford is a former mill village laying claim to one of the first mills that were built on the route of the Derwent. Over at Highlow Hall there is the main residence of the Eyre family, once the principal land-owners in the area. North Lees Hall was also owned by the Eyre family and it is said that William Eyre built a house for each of his sons within view of his own home.

Castleton, famous for its Blue John stone mined from spectacular caves, is a picturesque village that could have come straight off a Christmas card.

Many visitors to the area, seeing the spectacular scenery and the attractive villages, would be surprised to know that the area was once a hive of industrial activity. Far from being an idyllic place to live, less than two hundred years ago a pall of smoke hung over Hathersage making it difficult to see from one end of the village to the other. Workers in the needle and pin factories had short, hard lives; many of them had died by the time they were thirty, their lungs clogged with dust from the grinding of the steel.

After the Second World War farming thrived but the fortunes of farmers changed. The downward spiral in farming continues into the twenty-first century with the majority of farmers having to diversify to support their farms.

The coming of the Peak District National Park in 1951 had a major impact on the area. It now has the second largest number of visitors to any National Park in the world and the villages that are part of The Park have seen a massive growth in terms of tourism which provided and continues to provide economic prosperity.

Environmentally it was inevitable that the influx of visitors would effect the habitats of birds and animals. However, environmental work continues to attempt to balance the needs of the visitors with those of the environment and successes are seen each year.

The more recent history of the area is captured in this book in the words of local people and visitors to what must be one of the most beautiful areas of Britain.

Jenny Edgar, Literature Development Officer
Derbyshire County Council November 2003

LIFE AROUND STANAGE

A family name that is well known in the area is that of Priestley. The family came to Overstones in the seventeen-sixties when Samuel Priestley came to Hathersage from Manchester.

I was born in Jessops in Sheffield but my Dad assured me that I was made at Overstones in the front bedroom! Overstones was in the Priestley family from the seventeen-hundreds through to about 1986 or '87 when Uncle Peter retired. As you go down to the back door there's a gennel that's built into the house and there's a stone there that's got seventeen-sixty something on it. Apparently, it was built as a coaching place – they used to change the horses there. What made Samuel come here God knows. I don't.

My granddad and his brother, Septimus, the seventh son of the Priestley family, worked for the Duke of Rutland on Longshaw Estate. They were shepherds and they used to go up into the Yorkshire Dales to buy sheep for the Duke and then they'd drive them back from there. One of the stopping-off places was a place called Luddonden Foot, which is near Sowerby Bridge. They used to stay there overnight and that's where my granddad met my grandma. They married and my dad was born in 1898.

I know my grandfather, Ernest, was one of seven children. Then there was John Priestley who farmed at Stannington. George Priestley never did anything – he wasn't one hundred percent. Aunt Sarah eventually became Mrs White and Aunt Polly lived at Sharrowbottom – that's below Bilston, what's called Bilston Croft. There were two little cottages – I don't know whether they're still there – and she lived in one of them. Aunt Ann lived at Higgar Lodge, half way up Littlemore Road – she was called Mrs Higginson. Those cottages have gone now. Her husband worked in the quarries. Uncle Sep farmed at Parson House up above Fox House but before that he farmed at Strawberry Lea which is in the middle of Blackamoor. George Stone was above Fox House in a little cottage. He was a retired policeman turned game-keeper and he used to do a bit of farming for anybody who needed it. A little bit farther down, on the corner where the lay-by is, there used to be a cottage called Piper House. John Priestley, Uncle Sep's son, lived there and as he walked down the road he'd take two strides and his head'd go to one side. He'd take another two strides and his head'd go to the other side. 'He was nick-named Niddy Nod'.

We used to have parties and my mum and dad took me and my brother, Gerald, in the horse and trap. We'd go down to Whitehouse, where my grandma lived at the back of the Millstone Inn. And Chatsworth, where my dad was born. Not Chatsworth where the Duke of Devonshire is, there's a Chatsworth Cottage at Hathersage. Two children were born there, my Dad and Uncle John. Later they moved to Whitehouse where Aunty Edith and Uncle Ashton were born.

At that time the Moors, Stanage Moor and Moscar Moor and all round Overstones and White Path, belonged to Colonel Beecham. He owned North Lees and Snuffy Wilson, from the snuff manufacturers in Sheffield, owned Moscar and Stanage. Nobody was allowed on the Moors at week-ends. My dad and Peter used to spend hours on a Saturday and a Sunday keeping people off the moors.

They didn't want people up there because they thought the visitors would take the birds. They used to shoot and the first drive was Sheep Wash Bank, then you went across the road and drove from the backside of Stanage planting, what they called Buckstone, then they'd drive catching Sidemoor before they went to Overstones for lunch.

Peter would lunch in the living room and the gentry had their lunch in the sitting room. Tell you a story about that – it was the first time I ever got drunk! I could only just reach up to the table. The gentry had had theirs and they'd gone out. I went in the front room and I was going round drinking what was left in the glasses. My mother said I didn't wake up for three days!

After lunch, we walked over towards Sheffield and drove Bingham Moor all back again towards Burbage, and that's from Lady Cannon Planting, which is near Ringinglow. Next we'd walk right on the boundary, on White Path to Stanage, and drove back. End of the day – ten bob. It was a lot of money in those days. If you got a penny you were doing very well.

"Mr Ollerenshaw was at North Less. That was a poultry farm at that time with big hen houses. Every Friday morning he used to go with a pony and cart to Sheffield to sell his eggs and one Friday night at Overstones I heard a horse galloping down the road. One of the shafts was stuck in the harness – somebody had run into it with a motorbike at Ringinglow. The horse went back home. I can hear that horse now, galloping down the road and the shaft bouncing at the side."

Going back to Overstones; the farm is right up the Dale, under Stanage Rocks. There was no proper road to it, no mains water only rain water that was caught in the troughs where they used to water the cows. Our water used to come out of a spring and we had to carry it down.

It was a big community; there were the Ollerenshaws at North Lees and they had nine kids; there was Brookfield Manor – just at the back of the Manor House; there's a tiny little cottage that's being renovated now, ever so tiny – the Spittlehouses lived there. The Thorpes were at Kimber Court and they'd got a daughter, Pam. She was a cracker! And Muriel Hutchinson who is now Mrs Wilcoxson. The Miss Hodgkinsons were three spinsters who lived at Moorseats, one of the houses, along with North Lees, referred to in the novel 'Jane Eyre'. They were one of the first families in Hathersage and their brother lived at Carr Head and they had Carhead Moor. They used to shoot up there. There was Norman Priestley at Mitchell Field and Aunt Lucy, Peter's mother, at Callow. Reg Curtis and his two daughters and son lived at Leveret Croft and my Uncle Peter lived at Cattiside. He was a game-keeper on the Estate.

We used go to the rounds of parties at North Lees, Cattiside, Curtis's at Leveret's, Spittlehouses and Brookfield. There were big family gatherings and shearings. Everybody went to shear.

I was at Overstones shearing on the day the invasion started. My grand-dad had been killed in a road accident going from Overstones to a sheep dog trial at Ilam Bridge so my dad moved from Overstones in 1937 down to Whitehouse so that the dairy herd could be carried on for my grandma. He had an overhand in Hathersage but as soon as I could I would milk with my Dada and be late for school. That morning I was going up to Overstones and walked up the Dale with my dad. He went back home and I walked on.

I remember hearing on the radio about the invasion in France. Before that they dropped bombs on Hathersage, one on the rocks up the Dale, another in Norman's field. Clifford Priestley, he was Peter's brother and lived at Callow at that time, went out of the door and he saw Norman walking up to this hole where the bomb had dropped. He walked up and he walked round and he walked back again and just as he walked into the yard, the time-bomb went off! They dropped a lot of incendiaries around North Lees. One side was set on fire using incendiary bombs. There was a search light and big guns on Station Road, where the houses are now and the soldiers were billeted in the Memorial Hall and in the hotels in the village.

There were quite a few men that went to war and quite a few that never came back.

There were some killed who'd never gone away.

Bill Smith and Bill Crump, who lived on the Bank at Hathersage, used to go down to the Millstone to play dominos. Invariably they'd be the only ones in, especially during the war. They were down at Millstone playing dominoes one night when the Sheffield blitz was on. My dad used to go down nearly every night for a crafty pint and a game of dominos. This night he was going down the lane and he called out to Charlie Wiggett, who'd made an air-raid shelter for the Burgins, 'Now then, Charlie, are you coming down for a drink?'

'No' he said, 'they're bombing Sheffield, can't you hear 'em? I'm going in here.'

So Charlie went down in the air-raid shelter and my dad went down to the Millstone. They sat there drinking and in a bit a car pulls up outside

Sheep wash May 1927 at
Sheep Wash Bank
© Mr Middleton

and George Lawrence, who owned the 'Laurel' Razor Blade factory in Sheffield, comes in the pub.

'What you doing George?'

'I'm going to Sheffield.'

'There's a blitz in Sheffield, they're bombing Sheffield.'

You could see the glow in the sky, you could hear it.

He said 'No, I've got to go to work. The girls are working in the factory, I've got to go and see to them.'

He never came back.

Going back to shearing, one time, at Overstones, it had come on to drizzle. Everybody got together in those days, gave each other a hand.

Peter said 'Go in the house and have a cup of tea. I've got the sheep in, they're fairly dry.'

Anyway when he went into the shed, they weren't dry. So he took them out in the field and he ran them round. We decided the best way to spend the time was playing half-penny nap. So we got a nap school going. We played until four o'clock and Peter kept taking these sheep out to dry and fetching them back in. We started shearing at four and at eight o'clock we'd sheared them all and were playing nap again. They were all hand shears, there were no machines.

In my school days, when I started at the Top School, there was a Miss Stanton that taught the infants. She was one of those very strict ladies. When she left, Aunty Frances came. She'd been a pupil-teacher and I got on a lot better with her. She married Uncle Fred and they'd courted from school days, the two of them. She married him and he went in the RAF and flew in a Mosquito, him and a pilot. They used to go straffing trains over on the continent. He said 'You never need to worry about me, our aeroplane's made of wood, it'll float,' but it didn't. They shot him down over the North Sea and he's buried on the Isle of Iona.

It was a lovely school. Good cricketers, good footballers. If it became frosty the Headmaster'd help us to make a slide in the school yard. He was born in the Dale of Hathersage and he had two younger brothers. They all went into the forces together in 1939 when the war started – we were on holiday from school – and of course he'd gone when we got back. He'd been in the Territorials, you see, before the war. His brothers, Jack and Bob, were younger. He'd taught his brother Bob for a while and he was a great bloke – Harry Schofield. He'd give you the stick for something as soon as, but if you didn't do it again it was forgotten. He was as straight as a dye.

There was hardly a dry eye in Hathersage School that morning, when we went to school and realised he'd gone. He was in Dunkirk and his brother Jack was a Despatch Rider. One day Harry was just standing there and Jack came up on the motorbike.

Harry said to him, 'Have you seen Bob?'

'Well,' he said 'last time I saw him, two or three days ago, he was at such and such a place.'

'Well,' Harry said 'get on the motorbike and go and fetch him.'

And he did – and all three of them came back from Dunkirk together! He came back to teach in Hathersage School.

When you started in school, in the morning you'd have the assembly then he'd say to the lads 'Right, if you get your work done quickly, at lunchtime we'll either go up into the garden and do some gardening or we'll go and have a football match.' Harry could teach but when he went and a fellow from Heanor took his place he couldn't teach me anything. I just couldn't get on with him at all. It was a good job there was Sheila there. I was crackers about her.

I only found out, years and years after I'd got married; a group of us were talking and they said that Sheila was absolutely crackers on me and I never knew! I did get to take her home an odd time or two! My wife knows about her. I don't keep any secrets from my wife, except them that I don't want her to know!

Years later we used to go to Longshaw Sheep Dog Trials on the first Saturday in September and they held the flower show in Hathersage School. I went in this particular Saturday night and Harry was there.

He said 'How are you? Are you married?'

I said 'Yes.'

'Any children?'

'Yes – one and one on the way.'

There'd been a flower show on that particular Saturday. Harry used to be a big man at growing dahlias – it was his favourite job, gardening. And he picked a bunch of dahlias off the stand and said 'Give those to your wife.' It brought tears to my eyes, I tell you. A grand bloke – Harry. The last time I saw him he was in a pub in Bakewell and we had a drink together. He must have died about six months ago.

There were some characters about in those days.

Old Sam Eyre came up to my grandma's one day. He used to go buying sheep and walked them back and he'd invariably go back and get some more. Anyway, he came up to my grandma's at Whitehouse one day.

'Now then,' he said 'I'll just have a cup of tea.'

She makes him a cup of tea and Old Sam sits on this settle thing, chaise-longue you call them. He sat there drinking his tea and he says 'I'll just take me shoes off a bit.'

He was there for a week! It's true! Perfectly true!

One day my dad was walking over the Bank and Frank Wilson, who lived at Greenwood Farm, came running over.

'Eh up,' he said 'I've found a dead bloke on the straw stack.'

> **"One particular day at Fox House they were going to have a pigeon shoot and my granddad said 'There's no way I'm shooting pigeons, I've never had a gun on my shoulder and I'm not going to start'.**
>
> **Grandad said 'I'll tell you what I'll do. I'll give a fat weather for a Sheepdog Trial.'**
>
> **Apparently he'd been to Balla in North Wales and that was the first Sheep Dog Trial in the country.**
>
> **My dad only missed two Sheepdog Trials in his life at Longshaw. He went to the first one in September and he was born in November and he went to every other one except when he was ill around about 1979. And the trials are still going now. It will be the one hundred and fifth year this year."**

My dad said Frank was frightened to death over it. They went back, had a look and sure enough, this bloke was dead under the stack sheet. So they had to ring Hadfield, the policeman, up and he came up in his Morris 8 car. It had a carrier on the back. Old Hadfield had a look at this bloke and they established he wasn't local. Hadfield felt in his pocket and found five and sixpence so Old Hadfield put it in his own pocket.

My dad said 'What are we going to do now?'

'We're going to put him on the back of the car and take him to Johnny Thompson's mortuary.'

Johnny Thompson was the undertaker. They wrapped the body in the sack-sheet and fastened him on back of the car. Frank Wilson would have nothing to do with that, he was frightened to death. My dad went down with Old Hadfield and they were going past the Scotsman Pack Inn and saw Johnny Thompson's motorbike in the Scotsman's Yard.

'Johnny's in here. We'll go in the Scotsman's and drink this five and sixpence worth at the bar.'

In they go and Johnny says 'What are you buggers doing in here?'

'We've brought you a body.'

'Don't be so daft.'

'We have – it's outside on the back of the car.'

They went outside for Johnny to have a look then went back in again and bought Johnny a drink. But Albert Sunderland wouldn't serve Hadfield because he'd got his Police hat on!

There's plenty of stories about pubs and offies. James Bannaman had a one-stop shop, a beer-off, and he kept his beer in the cellar. He used to bring the beer up in jugs-full to serve people and he couldn't understand why a barrel had suddenly gone empty. He couldn't reckon it up. He went down the cellar one night and found Little David Cooper. That's where his beer was going. Little David was so drunk that he couldn't get out again!

At one time I knew everybody in the village but I don't know hardly anybody in my own village now at Hope or at Castleton. It's changed a lot and it changed very rapidly. The big change came when the Peak Park Planning Board, in their wisdom, decided that derelict farm buildings should be made into holiday cottages. That was one mistake the Peak Park made because it changed the whole population. The cottages in the villages have become 'Holiday Lets' and the prices have been inflated and the prices are now too expensive for the young people to afford. This was not as intended. There were four cottages for sale in Hathersage. There was one cottage, the one that's near the old Catholic school, that was only a little one. They reckoned it would make around about forty to fifty thousand. They started at fifty, then eighty. The youngsters from the village can't touch them.

When we left Overstones in 1937 Uncle Peter took the tenancy and moved from Cattiside with Auntie Maud, their young son Brian and Baby Rita. Uncle Peter was an excellent shepherd and managed Overstones very well. Once, when some sheep had got trapped on a ledge on the rocks, disregarding his own safety he climbed down to rescue them. If he'd lost his balance he would have fallen several feet and been badly injured and on his own. There were very few people about in those days and no mobile phones.

Another time, when there was a fire on the moor and he thought some sheep were surrounded, he walked into the fire and suffered serious burns to his feet as his boots caught alight.

He never learned to drive but he bought a car for Auntie Maud to drive. After the war he bought a small tractor with a carrier box on the back in which Auntie Maud rode sitting on a chair. Coming back from the village he stopped at the gate. 'Aren't you going to open the gate, Maud?' No reply! He went back and she was walking up the Dale. 'You clumsy B...,you tipped me out when you set off.' Another silent journey home!

He used to walk over the moor to Whitehouse and he and Dad went for a drink and a game of dominoes every Saturday night. The he would call for a cup of tea and a chat till gone midnight and then walk the two miles back home.

At that time the Priestley's occupied nearly all the farms on the Eastern side of Hathersage and Norman Priestley farmed at Mitchell Fields. He had a spinster sister called Florry who always asked 'How's your hens laying?'

His brother, John, was always called the 'Fiddling Farmer'; a virtuoso of the violin as was his wife and daughters. At the time there was an orchestra in the village and John was dissatisfied with the tuning of his violin. One of the other players, joking, said, 'Why don't you make one of your own?' and he did. He actually made four and they are in his grand-daughter's house in Bradwell to this day.

Until quite recently there was a brass band in the village. Years ago it was conducted by Uncle Peter's father, another Peter who was affection-ately nicknamed 'Choppam' as he always told the players to cut the notes off short.

I don't live at Overstones now. I live in Hope – in all ways!

Ron Priestley

Like Ron Priestley, Ray Platts was from a farming family and Ray has a fund of stories about the people and places in the Stanage area.

I was born in Hathersage but I left when I was seventeen or eighteen. My father, John, was a farmer and milkman. He always wore breeches and leggings and the leggings were polished up until you could see your face in them.

I had an uncle, John Charles Platts, who was very short tempered. My grandfather used to collect the taxes around here and when he left farming Uncle John Charles took on the collecting. It was a bit of a push to keep the farm work, the milk round and the collecting going. He delivered milk to one woman who was never up and he always had to wash a jug or a basin to put the milk in. One hay-time he was so desperate to get back to his hay that he went in this woman's house and shouted for something to put the milk in.

She called back, 'Well, can *you* find something?'

'Yes', he called back, got the colander that was in the middle of the table and poured the milk into it!

He said there was always something to put it in after that.

There were six milkmen in the area, ourselves, the Priestleys, the Helliwells, Swindells, Elliots and Mothams.

All the farmers had their own milk so we just went round the village. Any that we didn't sell there went to wholesale. Before the Milk Marketing Board came along any surplus was made into butter. You had butter when there was a lot of milk around and you went without when there wasn't. You had dripping or bread and jam.

There was a fair that came to the village in October. There was always a roundabout and swings. It's funny what sticks in your mind. There was a chappy selling boiled sweets and I had met Uncle John Charles, who always carried his money in a purse. He always had a sovereign or two in those days. After a lot of rooting he gave me a penny. Now we didn't get a penny in a month. So I went to this stall and I wanted a pennyworth of sweets and he gave me halfpence worth. He said I'd only given him a half-penny. And I've never forgotten it.

There's people from those days that stick in your mind. Old Prince was one of them. He was a stone-waller. It didn't matter if he were building a gap up Upperidge Way or a house in Hathersage; if you asked him what time it was he could stand back off his wall and he'd tell you, within ten minutes, what the time was. That's always beaten me because building a wall is never that simple. Some days you can get on and some days you can't.

There was Johnny Thompson, who was a joiner and undertaker. He called a spade a spade and he didn't mind whether it was a Duchess or a Duke. He took snuff and my dad used to take some as well. My mother used to say my dad took that much that his brains'd turn to parkin!

"Old Ben Rose, who used to do all the slaughtering for the butchers, used to take bets that he could kill, skin and dress a lamb whilst Hathersage Church clock struck twelve. And that's how he earned his lunch!"

I remember Johnny putting a window in and he had this lad, an apprentice I suppose he was, on the outside. Johnny was on the inside because it was raining, of course, and he got this lad knocking a peg into the hole. The lad missed the peg and caught Johnny through with a hammer. Old Johnny yelled 'That were nearly my nose!'

There was a chap who went round the farms working a bit. Mills he was called but I can't think of his Christian name. He was really a tramp, he slept anywhere. He always had this very thick hazel stick and if you shouted 'Gee' to him, he'd give you a great whacking.

Every year there was a fair in the village and a circus on Bannerman's Field on Station Road. Our local policeman was Bobby Walker and they always brought an extra one in for the summer. This particular year it was a young Irishman. There were some youths that were playing heck. They got on the roundabouts and this Irish bobby jumped on and threw them both off. Just threw them off as they were going round. He collared them and banged their heads together and marched them down Station Road and chucked them in the lock-up. But you see that settled it. They didn't take them to court as they do now. They scufted them and you went back home and said 'Bobby Walker's hit me, dad' and then your dad hit you too!

Old Blagden was another one from the village. He had a horse and cart and he used to empty all the bins and that sort of thing. There was a lady who lived at the last house going out of Hathersage, beyond the railway bridge. She was very big in the Wesleyan Church so she was very fortunate to get a cottage right next to the Old Chapel. When she moved in she got Mr Blagden to remove her. He borrowed our four-wheel wagon and he started about 7.00 o'clock in the morning, flitting this woman and all her belongings. When it got to about 3.00 o'clock, she said 'Well, I think there's only one load left now Mr Blagden, so I'll stop here and make a cup of tea.'

He said 'Thank you very much.'

So he brought this last load and she poured this tea out and she said 'Would you like something to eat?'

He said 'Oh yes, I wouldn't mind.'

She said 'Well, could you eat an egg?'

And he said 'Oh aye and the bloody ham as well!

The Spittlehouse children were brought up at Birley Farm in the '50's and '60's.

We had a lovely childhood roaming around the countryside. One of our favourite places was The Warren which is just across the fields from North Lees. It has beautiful woodland walks, a pond, a waterfall and a ruined paper-mill. We could take a picnic and paddle all day.

One day one of us got a bit too wet and went to see Aunty Muriel (Prigent) for help with drying out. Usually we were given a drink and a piece of home made cake.

We sometimes went to North Lees anyway, our parents were friendly and would help with gathering and shearing. They also went out together on special occasions. The Prigents had four children, two of them older than us and two younger, who might be around too. In those days the Hall was a ruin, you could see between the floor boards and hens were kept on the first floor. The ground floor was a dumping ground but the beautiful ceilings were in evidence then.

Occasionally, under supervision, we went up to the roof to admire the view.

Carl Wark
© Peak District National Park Authority

The ruins of the Chapel
© Robert Helliwell

Our Dad used to farm sheep and built a wall around Sheepfold Field at Sandy Lea and also had some sheep pens in there so that they could be contained when they needed worming. We all had to help, along with the dogs.

Sandy Lea was also popular with us because a stream ran through it and we would take a picnic up there. All generations of the family would go and we'd find a flat, grassy patch and eat and paddle till home time. Everybody enjoyed the welcome relaxation time.

One very hot summer, when we'd had no rain, the water supply dried up. In those days the water came from a stream drained into a brick-built tank across the road from Birley Farm. So we ended up taking milk churns in the old Landrover to bring water down to the farm. The churns were filled from the stream round Sandy Lea. It must have been a time-consuming task.

In the late '60's the Hall was renovated and the Prigents started having paying guests. They also put on wedding receptions and my brother and sister had their receptions there.

We always understood there was an underground passage from the ruined chapel to North Lees although we never saw any evidence of it.

Lynn Ellis and Dianna Ackerman

Roger Watson has more idea than most people about how Stanage and the surrounding area has developed over the years. Born at Bank Cottages, behind what was the Westminster Bank, he has continued to live, work and walk in the area all his life.

I don't have much recollection of living at Bank Cottages because my family moved to Baulk Lane, which is the general path that everybody uses to go to Stanage from the village.

It was a quiet place to grow up, nothing too exciting, just village activities; Scouts, that type of thing.

We all used to play at the Hood Brook, by Stanage Edge. It's the main brook that runs up the valley. We'd go off for days, nobody would bother us at all. We didn't take picnics or anything, we'd just go. Then children could go where they liked, more or less.

I went to the Top School, the same as Ron Priestley, and some of the teachers that taught him, taught me. I don't think the Head teacher, Harry Schofield, was as well-loved on our side of the war as at Ron's. He was very regimental; we used to have to line up and march into school. The army might have had that sort of influence on him. He was very strict and did a lot of shouting. Very much the Sergeant Major.

There was only the Catholic school at the bottom of the village and the Top School, which was Church of England, so we just carried on in the same school until we were old enough to go to work. I was fifteen when I left and I didn't go far away. I worked in Bradwell, only five miles down the road, all my working life.

I worked for a little engineering company and they provided transport for us. Occasionally, when we had to work nights and there were only two or three of us on the shift, we'd have to provide our own transport and that was usually a push-bike.

When the weather was bad five miles could feel quite a long way in the snow but there's only been a few times that I haven't been able to get in. It's not all that far to walk. It was part of the pleasure of the job, I suppose. A bit of a challenge to get there.

The village has changed over the years. There's certainly a lot more people living here that are strangers to the area. Because we're in the Peak Park you can't build new houses to any great extent. The ones that are here are more sought after, so the price of houses keeps going up. It's had a big effect on younger people because unless they can get work they've not been able to stay in the village, and even then they can't afford the houses. Sheffield is the cheapest place to go but it must be a bit of a shock after Hathersage.

One of the biggest changes is that the ones who come in are the ones who are more interested in committees and organising anything locally. The locals tend to let things slide by.

I think there's less people walking on Stanage than there used to be. When everyone came on the trains there'd be streams of walkers about.

Millstones in the snow
© Robert Helliwell

We get plenty of people walking now but in smaller parties. They just get the car and go.

The fact that people have more money around has made a difference too. It's easier for them to get out, they don't rely on public transport and where we used to wear ex-army stuff it's all specialised gear nowadays.

Because Stanage is so close to Sheffield we get a lot of students coming out walking and climbing. People even come up from London, sometimes just for the day, because the Peaks are the nearest hills to London.

There's more people running bed and breakfasts than there used to be. I think it's only in the last ten or fifteen years that people have started taking visitors and farmers have taken up the idea of converting a few barns for accommodation for walkers and visitors – parties of visitors especially.

Farms change what they do. A lot of farmers always used to have a field of potatoes, but you hardly see any now. They're better grown in other parts of the country. They'd grow corn but you don't see a lot of it now – it's mostly sheep.

I appreciate the area. It's a pleasant place and on my doorstep, too. For me, Stanage is a fairly regular stomping ground.

Roger Watson

What happens when you've lived in an area nearly all your life, feel it is part of you, carry it in your bones but are no longer able to live alone? For Nell Frost, Mary Marshall, Eileen Robinson and Tom Armitage, Gernon Manor in Bakewell is the answer; not too far from their roots and a place where they can be sure of finding someone else who enjoys talking about the old days in their particular area of the Peak District.

Hathersage? It's one of the best places on earth. I am Nell, I'm eighty-nine and I was born and bred there.

My mother died of her 10th child when she was only forty and left eight of us. The first child died and the youngest was a year old when she died. My sister, Evelyn, who had to look after us, was only seventeen. She's still living. Unfortunately, when my mother died Dr Holbrook was away on holiday, the first time he'd been away for years. He was very upset about it because he said if they'd got her into hospital a day before they could have saved her life. The baby died too.

It made us all independent, we had to be. I was fourteen and we left school at that age. We had to go to New Mills for an exam when we got to that age. One of us passed and went on to be the head of Edale School. I think that was the only one who passed. The others looked upon it as a day out.

My dad, John Thomas Thompson, was joiner, builder, decorator, under-taker, everything under the sun. He thought he was it!

We had a house called the 'Hearse House' where they kept the dray for funerals but unfortunately they've demolished it. But Dad didn't have a horse for funerals. As far as I can remember he had a hearse from Sheffield.

There'll be some people who remember him.

You can imagine my mother doing the washing for eight children. Two was enough for me! She had a copper outside, in a wash-house. It didn't matter what the weather was like, I've worked in the wash-house when the mangle rollers have frozen.

We always dried the clothes outside on lines across the yard. One part was Mrs Wilson's, the next was ours and we never trespassed on one another's washing line.

We had a bath every week. Religiously, ever week.

We had to share the outside toilet and one day my mother went in such a big hurry she sat on the next-door-neighbour's knee! And it was a man! There were eight of us and the next-door-neighbours had eight, all men, but we all shared the same toilet.

We never had to buy any vegetables, we had a big garden and grew all of them. And we had two pigs for meat.

The milk came in churns and was poured into a measure then into our jug. My mother baked all her own bread for the eight of us. She wouldn't have dreamed of buying bread. She'd leave it rising in the pancheon then put it in the oven that was in our sitting-room. A range. The fender had roses on it. All black leaded.

There was a lamp-lighter in the village. Every evening he'd go round with a taper to light the gas lamps but I don't know if he came to turn them off in the morning.

Window-tapping – that's what we did; fastened a pin to the putty, and something that would tap the window, then get ready to run when they came to the door. We've broken a window many a time with tapping.

My schooldays were very, very happy. We never thought of falling out. Mr Roden, our schoolmaster, had been there years and years and he believed in caning. I was sat in the front row one day and I got the tail end of the cane and I hadn't done anything. And oh, goodness, it did hurt. One boy was always late because he had to walk a good mile, or even two miles. He used to get the cane and sulk through the lesson.

The next schoolmaster was a very young man and he burnt all the canes. He had more discipline without them than the one with them. He made some of the pupils prefects and I was one of them. We each had a job to do every week and then we changed them over. We thought we were it! One of my jobs was looking after Little John's grave in Hathersage churchyard.

Mr Roden's daughter was the primary school teacher. She was late by half-an-hour every morning but it was her father who was the boss so it didn't matter. Of course, she had to pull her socks up when the new teacher came.

I don't know what they do now but then we had to learn our tables off by heart.

When they got a canteen we could stay for our dinner. For a lot of us that was the only hot meal of the day and at one time we got free milk.

On Sundays we got dressed in our best things, all white, and went to Sunday School in the morning and Catechism in the afternoon. Sunday was taken up.

I was the officer that used to stick the Sunday school stamps in the books. I liked them, they were nice, very colourful. We got a prize if we filled a full book and a prize for attendance.

Mine was 'A Hundred Puddings and Spices' – something like that. I always wanted to be a cook. It was my ambition.

The churches in Hathersage are very united, always have been. The church and chapel-goers and the Roman Catholics often have services in each others churches. It's not like that everywhere.

There wasn't any choice as to what we'd do when we left school. When I left my Dad said 'You're not wearing a cap and apron for anybody.' Of course, he had to change his mind, I wouldn't have had a job. Practically all of us went into service and I was parlour-maid at Nether Hall.

Every drop of water had to be pumped and every so often it ran dry and I had to pour some down to get some back. Now I think 'However did I do it?'

I was seventeen when I started and I didn't particularly like it until I came to work for the local doctor. He and his wife were marvellous to me. Dr Holbrook was much loved by villagers.

In those days the doctors made their own medicine – half-a-crown a bottle. People would come to the door for them and I'd pass them out to them. One day I was put in a predicament because the doctor said 'Nellie, don't let these people have their medicine unless they pay for it.' That was the one and only time he ever said that.

I worked for him for five years. It was the best job I've ever had.

Before I got married I used to love dancing. I went out with Ashton Priestley – I know what you're going to say Tom – 'Who didn't?' – and I went to a dance and he was there but he might never have known me. He came to meet me the next night and I said 'What do you think I am?' I thought, the cheek of it! I told him to take himself off. If I wasn't good enough to dance with then I didn't want to know him. And off I went and left him. He'd taken another woman, that was the trouble. And he was meant to be going out with me. He was a bit of a lad!

They were lovely dances; the Waltzes, Slow Foxtrot, Lambeth Walk, Oi!

On one of the cards that I had on my 21st birthday it said 'Don't forget the Slow Foxtrot tonight!' I was a good dancer.

My father had a motor-bike and side-car and he took seven of us to dances. One night he said 'Our Nell's not going.' But I went. He used to go out to the pub and I went then.

I got married in 1939 when I was twenty-four and my husband was twenty-eight. I've said the churches were always united but that didn't stop my father turning me out when he knew my husband-to-be was a

Catholic. To him Catholics were Catholics and Protestants were Protestants and they shouldn't marry. 'I shall not give you away and you'll never come in this house again.' That's what he said. He didn't even come to the wedding so I didn't have a parent with me because my mother was dead. He soon forgave me but it was difficult for a short time.

We got married on three pounds a week and I've never owed a penny in my life. That was an average wage to keep two of us and we lived quite comfortably on it.

We lived at Sunny Side Cottage; one tap with cold water, one gas ring and stone flag floors. But we managed.

Later on we improved on the gas ring. I got a gas cooker that my husband played pop about. Said it was far too much for a working man but I got it just the same.

I was the world's worst fire-lighter. We made paper sticks or went out 'sticking', getting twigs and branches to push underneath. But it never worked so I poured paraffin on it and dropped a match in it. I was surprised to see the stove was still there. And it burned my hair and brought some soot down. I never did it again!

I used to hold a sheet of paper in front of the fire then it'd catch light and I'd have to move quickly to put it out!

Nell Frost

Mary Marshall, who is ninety-eight years old, wasn't born in the Stanage area but has lived there so long she considers herself a local. Mary nursed in Sheffield before moving to Bradwell when she married.

We lived at Bradda in a farm right on top of the hill. It was lovely, you could see so far. I liked living on top of the hill, it's just difficult, when you get older, to get up and down it.

I married a man from Bradwell that I met at a dance. I was working in London at that time and my husband, before we were married, used to come every weekend to see me. Soft as a brush!

Before that I used to go out with one of the Hancock's boys. The

Hancock's lived at Bamford and had shops in all the villages. When I was going out with Aaron sweets were very scarce. It was almost impossible to get any and he used to bring me a bar of chocolate every time I saw him.

Being a housewife was hard work, the women worked harder than the men. Coal was tipped outside the house and had to be shovelled into the coal house. The front of it was level with the farmhouse but the back was high up so they tipped the coal there and it only needed shovelling down, pulling forward. We didn't use much coal though because we had our own wood and burned that. The only problem was that it was swift burning.

We used long pieces of wood to push under the oven. That's going back a bit. We had a steel fender that went right round and we'd put lambs under that to keep them warm until the sheep had had all of her lambs. Then they went back to her. When I was back home in Yorkshire we had a cade lamb that we brought up, called Nancy. When she had her lambs my eldest brother said 'We'll take Nancy a long way away then she'll not bother us.'

He took her to a field we had about four miles away but she turned up back at the house with her four lambs. My mother said 'Nancy's not going away again.'

Nancy and the lambs were clean in the house; they'd trained themselves and they never made a mess.

Dinner was the main meal of the day and the men wanted it ready and waiting when they came home at night.

There was the washing to do, baking the bread – everything was baked, cakes, jams, everything. It was no good running out of anything because it was miles from the shop.

The ironing was a chore, heating up irons by the fire. Took ages.

But they were good old days.

Mary Marshall

Eileen Robinson was born in Midland Cottages, Grindleford.

My family name is Giles and my dad, William Robert Giles, was a signalman. Lovely fellow. He came from Bournemouth in Dorset and came up with the railway because they had to go wherever they were sent. Unfortunately, he broke his hand and couldn't continue being a guard so he had to go into the signal box and work there till his retirement. Mum was from Ecclesfield, the other side of Sheffield.

I had one brother and two sisters, all of them older than me.

From when I was five I had a mile to walk to school, from Grindleford Station right down to the village, even in snow.

I'm glad to say I was good so I never had the cane. But I must have been naughty at home sometimes because I'd always be put in the pantry. I didn't mind that. If the jars of jam were open I used to dip a finger in. If the condensed milk was open I thought I was in heaven. I loved it.

I was the one who had to go into the wash-house and heat the water for our bath. It took ages. Eventually we stopped bathing in front of the fire and bathed in the wash-house. We thought 'Why carry it?'

Washday really did take all day. We'd dry our clothes on the rack then, when they were ironed, we put them up again to air. No airing cupboards then.

My mother always baked our bread, in fact she won a prize for bread-baking. The smell as you walked into the house. Joyous.

The fire had to be alight in the morning to heat the water for a cup of tea. We always used coal but I've sawn logs for hours and hours. I loved sawing logs. It's the smell that comes off the wood.

Central heating's nice but it's far nicer to see a coal fire, isn't it? My husband worked on shifts so he'd light the fire. It was lovely to come down to.

In my early teens I went into service and had to walk a mile there and a mile home every night.

I had to help kill the cockerels. I didn't like doing it but if someone rang up for a chicken I had to go and get one and kill it.

I thought the milk from cows that had just calved was special. It was called 'beastings' and it used to make lovely custard.

It's funny, I've never seen a lamb being born. Never. I've stood in the field waiting for a lamb to arrive but it hasn't and I've had to walk off and get on.

When I was a young girl I loved dancing. I loved the Palais Glide. There was a ballroom at The Maynard Hotel on the top of the hill and my brother-in-law, George Mullins, played in the band. He always made sure they played the Palais Glide for me.

One and six we paid to go in. It doesn't sound much but we were only earning three pounds a week.

Was life better then? It was harder work but I loved it.

Eileen Robinson

How many men went off to war and came back with a bride, particularly one who's been proposed to by someone else? That's what happened to Tom Armitage.

I didn't volunteer but I was called up and went straight out to France. And I came back with a French wife!

I went with the Militia to Belgium, Holland, Ceylon, India, Burma but it was in France that I met and married Charlene. I had an interpreter at the wedding. I'd met a lad who spoke good French so he spoke for me. He even proposed for me! Charlene came back to England later on. She liked England.

Our daughter's called Francine and I've a son called Mervyn Walter. Very English names!

Tom Armitage

Tom Armitage's war began over sixty years ago but one Sheffield resident was involved in a much earlier war. Whilst Tom left Bradwell to fight, Bill Sanderson return to a Bradwell in Roman Times. His daughter, Margaret Sanderson, tells his story:

My father lived on Ringstead Crescent, Sheffield, which is quite close to the old Roman road that leads over to Redmires and Stanage Edge.

One very wet afternoon I found him sitting in his usual chair looking out on his garden. He was feeling very frustrated as he was anxious to get on with his gardening but as soon as he got outside the heavens opened, so depriving him of his favourite occupation.

Then he asked 'What did the Romans do in Stannington?'

He knew of the Roman road and that Romans would have passed that way on the road into Derbyshire. Then he told me of a curious thing that had happened to him just before I arrived.

He was looking out of the window, hoping that the rain would stop, when he was very surprised to find that his garden had disappeared, along with all the neighbouring houses, and he seemed to be on open moorland. Then he saw a group of Roman soldiers making camp for the night. He said that he knew what they were doing as he had done it himself as a Coldstream Guardsman in the First World War. They were lighting fires and cooking food before settling down for the night. He said they did not look like the pictures of clean and smart Roman soldiers that you saw in books. They were exhausted and bedraggled.

He noticed two soldiers had moved away from the rest and were talking together. He knew that they were the commanding officers and that they were speaking in a foreign language but he knew what they were discussing. They were pointing to the opposite hillside to the north and instead of carrying on up the old road to Stanage they were going to strike out across Rivelin Valley to Stannington.

Then everything disappeared and returned to normal, leaving him very perplexed.

My father was a very sensible and logical man until the day he died and was not in any way given to vivid flights of fancy. He'd always been very sceptical about paranormal experiences and was certain he was not dreaming.

All this happened in the early 1970's and after he died I came across the booklet 'Prehistoric and Roman Times in the Sheffield Area', published by Sheffield City Museums. It mentions the find at Stannington of a bronze diploma of an auxiliary soldier from 124AD of which there is a copy in Weston Park Museum. I like to think that my father had, in some way, captured a scene from Roman times of soldiers on their bleak journey from Templeborough to Navio, Near Bradwell.

Margaret Sanderson

Generations of Mary Bailey's family have lived at Kimber Court with, as Mary puts it, Stanage as their back garden, their 'rockery'. The people who lived 'on the hill' may not have been blood relatives but they had a connection, a thread that ran through them, that made them dependent on each other. When tragedy struck Mary's family that thread was her life-line.

I was a February baby and my mother was thirty-nine when she had me, her first child. Because of the time of year and the fact that she was a bit old to be having babies I was born in Hathersage. When my mother died in childbirth six years later I went to live with my godmother, Enid Hodgkinson, who lived at Moorseats with her two sisters. They came to live here around 1912 and were quite an eccentric, exciting family. There were three boys and three girls; one son came home from boarding school and said he was ill but nobody believed him and he died. Cedric was killed during the 1st World War and Captain Geoffrey was a captain in the Home Guards. He was quite a character.

The eldest sister, Vera, was always known as Miss Hodgkinson. The second one, my godmother, Miss Enid, was a stalwart of the W.I. She was very keen on the Hucklow Players, dramas and books and during the winter months she just read plays. Miss Monica, the youngest sister, was a staunch Conservative but always wore a red hat. Loved everybody, loved the working man and would thump everybody on the back and say 'How are you today? I'm absolutely champion. How are you?'

She was so amazing and she got her OBE for services to the Conservative Party.

When my mother died I was taken to their house for them to look after me for the day and I just stayed. They did try to look after me but that was a bit difficult. They had this desperate task of trying to explain to me that my mother wasn't there anymore. It's a day I would never, ever want to re-live. I can remember every little bit of it from start to finish. To have a baby at the end of the day and no mother was something I just couldn't understand. I couldn't cope with that for a long time.

I used to sneak out to try to get up to the farm where I'd go through all the cupboards, the drawers, hidey-holes, everywhere, looking for my mother. It was absolutely a horrible time. In the end Miss Hodgkinson decided to take me down to the churchyard. As soon as I got down there I started trying to dig my mother up. It was rather horrible.

Miss Enid was very, very strict with me and she used to just call me 'Child'. It was as though I never had a name when I was a little girl. 'Child. Where's the Child?' 'Are you looking after the Child?' 'Where's she gone, the Child?'

Then there was the heartbreak when father had to sell the farm.

But there were compensations. My joy was that my mother's younger brother, Roly, sort of lived with us. He was such a character. He could make anything, he could do anything and he made life fun for me. He always had a car, a very nice car, and so we could go off and I always felt, as a child, that I'd lost other things but I had got bonuses.

He would go and buy a chicken hut and erect it and I would think 'This will make a nice play house.' So instead of having it as a chicken hut I had it as my play-house. I used to sleep in it because nobody ever worried about wandering around on the hillside. They used to put me in quite brightly coloured clothes, so that, as I'd got white-blonde hair, they could always see me.

I had a few frights though. One day I came across the back fields and I'd got some new shoes on. This person was walking towards me and, in this day and age it sounds awful, he was a black man with a turban on. I looked at him and no words would come out of my mouth. I shot home, trying to tell the family what I'd seen. This was the first time I'd ever seen somebody who wasn't like me. It frightened me to death. He was the Betta-Wear man, selling brushes. I tried to explain what I'd seen and in the end I fetched my golly and said 'This is what he's like.'

Every February, around my birthday, my father would find me a cade lamb. I accepted that at the end of the year it would go and I'd have another one. It used to go to the cricket matches with me and on walks on Stanage along with all the other animals. We didn't get many days holiday but always, on the 12th of August, all of us on the hillside would go for a picnic. My granny, who lived with us, was a most amazing cook. When pigs were killed there was never any waste. She'd make for everybody on the hillside; we had the black pudding, the dripping, the hazelet so she was usually in charge of making a wonderful picnic.

In the late nineteen-forties we had a new vicar, Vicar Fairclough. Miss Enid said 'We must invite the new vicar and his family up and we'll have this picnic on the moors'. It was a beautiful day and they came up and had this picnic and, of course, Mary had to take her pet lamb. And all sorts of my other pets went up as well. I think I was in a little bit of trouble because the lamb – I can't remember its name – had got its foot into all sorts of things and chaos ruled!

The weather's always been a challenge up here. Going way back to 1947 when we had that amazing snow, on the morning of the 29th or 30th January the butcher came up to collect a pig. He'd walked up but we couldn't get out because the gennel at the back of the house was full of snow. My father lifted me through the window and Asa Littlewood, the butcher, collected me the other side.

My father had to go out at all times to feed the animals, to go up on Stanage to collect sheep if he couldn't account for them. It was vital that you knew where every single animal was because it was an asset. Wealth wasn't like it is today – everything counted and mattered. He'd bring them in on his shoulders and put them in front of the kitchen stove to warm up.

Later on, in the summer, there was a gathering of farmers for the sheep dip. It was a real social occasion. Once the sheep had been sheared they had to be dipped. It was a legal requirement and our local policeman, PC Kirby, who was my friend's father, had to oversee the operation.

Our water comes from Leveret's Spring, so called because there are a lot of hares up there, and that never froze but the trough of water would freeze over and the icicles were two or three feet long. It was incredible. Even the milk in the dairy froze.

Although it was a really hard time and the snow was incredible all my thoughts are happy ones because it was such fun.

My grandmother made butter from the cream off the top of the milk and I'd go out on my pony, with my father on his big horse, taking the butter out to different families. We went on the top lane, over to Priestley's at Overstones, down to the other Priestley's at Cattiside then down to Mitchell Field to the other Priestleys – three lots of Priestleys.

Being a farming family the end of the summer was an interesting time. I loved harvest and hay-making. It was damned hard work for the men. My father used to have the young lads come in to help a bit. I loved drinking tea in the hay-field; it tasted wonderful.

Harvest Thanksgiving at church is always followed by a wonderful Harvest Supper. I'm quite obsessed by the moon and have been since I was a child. One year I was coming from the Harvest Supper and was walking up the lane, right at the bottom, and I was looking up at the moon. I walked round the corner and, of course, the moon had moved position. I fell over this thing in the middle of the lane and it was a prisoner-of war.

I said 'Oh my goodness' and my granny said 'Leave him be. Just leave him resting there and come on and forget about it.' But I've never forgotten about it. Every harvest or when I walk down the lane and it's windy or whatever, I always think about that poor chap lying there.

The prisoners-of-war used to march past Carr Head, Moorseats and Kimber on their way to the quarry on Carr Head Rocks. I'd hear them marching on the sandy cobbles and I was petrified of them. I don't know why because I didn't know what they were or who they were but I think it was the sound. I used to go and hide. They came down around four o'clock or five of an afternoon and I always had to hide in the horseradish. Now, I'm talking about when I was three or four. Horseradish was enormous to me. I used to get into this little nest. How can you explain to a child what it's about and why these people had to go up there?

We always had to listen to the news at mid-day or one o'clock after 'Workers Playtime' or 'Have a Go Joe' and again at six o'clock at night. That's all we were allowed to listen to – the news. It was all to do with this thing called 'The War' and I didn't know what it was all about.

When I grew up I moved away for a while before returning in 1963 when I married and came to live at Carr Head, and the Misses Hodgkinson were still my neighbours. I was getting to the stage of looking after them as they'd looked after me.

In the '70's we had an amazing winter where we got hoar frost with icicles. It only happened that once, we've never had a frost like that since. Because the old and woody branches on the trees were brought down by the weight of the icicles it was like a natural gleaning. It was devastation.

Monica rang up to see if I'd got something and I said I'd go along.

She said 'Oh no, don't Child, because the icicles could kill you.'

I said 'Well, I'm coming along right now.'

'Right. Well if you do you could just help me de-bark some branches to put them in the field for the rabbits, because the rabbits are dying.'

So we had to collect all these branches and make sort of things in the field so the rabbits had got some bark or something to eat. It didn't matter what we'd got to eat or what we hadn't got to eat.

Then when it was time for me to go home she said 'Oh, Child. You'll get killed on the way back.'

By this time I'd got my own children but I was still 'Child'.

Miss Monica always had a car and drove but latterly she'd say to me 'Now Mary, could you just take me somewhere?'

Half the time I hadn't got a license but I used to take her. I had an old Landrover and I think even the local policeman thought I'd passed my test, but I never did.

One day she said 'Mary, will you take me to Broomhill? I've got to see Claude Price because I want a new suit.'

So I said 'Yes, Miss Monica.'

We set off, going round and up Stanage, and she said 'Stop. Stop the car.'

So we stopped and looked out and she said 'Isn't that absolutely wonderful?'

Off we went to Claude Price at Broomhill. 'Morning Miss Monica, how are you?'

She said 'Claude, I want a suit the colour of the moors at twelve o'clock today.'

And he said 'You'll mean the Donegal Tweed, Miss Monica.'

'Something like that,' she said. ' A bit of heather, a bit of sludge and a bit of bracken.'

Sometimes she'd invite our local MP up for lunch and it was a question of 'Mary, have you got time to make something quickly?'

Sometimes, if I hadn't, she used to whisk up an Angel Delight, put a bit of cream with it, some strawberries and raspberries and Mr Wakefield always used to say 'Oh, Miss Monica, what a delightful sweet you've made. Absolutely.'

'I've been making it all morning!' she'd say. She could cheat like the rest of us.

They lived at Moorseats from 1912 to the 1970's and in all that time everything stayed in the same place as their mother had put it. They had it decorated and in the summer they had their chintzes at the windows and in the winter they had big blanket curtains but the furniture never moved. The china, the ornaments, the pictures were exactly the same. It was wrapped up in time. It was magic.

In the hall they had cases of butterflies. I know people would be horrified now but the colours were beautiful. Fluorescent. I actually loved them. There were boxes of stuffed birds. One was an albino pheasant which I desperately wanted but everything went into a sale when the house was sold. It was such a pity.

The old scullery had a mangle that I've still got in the garden as a curiosity. That was what they used for their clothes. They never got into a modern washing machine, not even in the '70's. They had an old stone sink with 'dollies'.

I was very lucky because I could just walk into their home but they were not familiar with people. The Aga man had to visit to service their Aga but they weren't very fond of him. They used to hide when he came and leave it to someone else to sort out. He was a smoker and had two cigarettes going all the time. I don't think he lasted too long into retirement, poor chap.

They didn't socialise much, except when, occasionally, they'd have the Bronte Society there. Miss Enid was into her dramas and she loved the

Bronte connection. She wanted to leave the house to the Bronte Society but, sadly, she was the first to die out of the three sisters and the others decided to sell it off. It was the end of an incredible era and the start of amazing changes on the hillside.

We used to own all the big moor until Captain Geoffrey persuaded members of the family to sell him the moor in the 1940's. They always said if he'd finished with it they'd have it back. So when the Hodgkinsons decided to go I said I'd really like to bring the moor back into Carr Head hands. Not that we want to use it as a moor but I felt I could look after it better than anyone else.

Miss Monica said 'Oh, no, Mary, you couldn't. The responsibility of looking after that – you're father's dead. Now he would have built the walls up. No, no. no. I'm going to leave it to the Peak District National Park.' She bequeathed it to them and they took it over but I really do wish we hadn't lost it.

"The area is just so beautiful. For many years I worked in Italy and I thought that was beautiful but this is even more so. There's a freshness about it, isn't there?"

And we still do have a picnic on the moors on 12th August but it's usually just our family and my nice neighbours will probably go up there with us.

We now get on a quaddy-bike and put all the picnic in the back of the trailer of the quaddy-bike – oh, that's awful. I didn't admit to that. I walk up.

And I still have my pet lambs. I'm not called Mary for nothing. I've got five of them in the field. They're always somebody else's who says 'I can't be doing with this.'

Nigel Dalton, the farmer over there, had one a few years back and he said 'The only person who'll look after this is Mary'.

He rang up and I said 'No, no Nigel. I'm not having another lamb in the kitchen, I'm trying to get my kitchen a bit more respectable.'

'No, no, no,' he said ' you'll have to have it and you'll put it in the oven

The Hodgkinson family
© Mary Bailey

Mary with Bunty in the 1962/3 snows
© Mary Bailey

and give it some brandy.'

Before I put the phone down my husband and daughter had gone to fetch it. It was like a bloody mule, this thing. It was the smallest little thing I've ever reared but it's still going strong and I think it must be about eight now. Harold is going to be thirteen, he's the eldest. He's got a bit of arthritis but he's all right. They go in the car with me. I used to take them to sales and to school and cause chaos. The children love it. Sometimes they go through the village and to the cricket. One went through the Hathersage Inn, got into the kitchens and sent things flying.

"Banty Hall Cottage was so isolated that years ago, when there was an old lady living there alone, somebody used to post her a magazine so that the postman would call once a month to check that she was all right."

My daughter took one to the Hathersage Gala and that went to the Hathersage Inn as well. We have a reputation!

As well as our picnic in August my husband and I go up on Stanage on New Years Eve. If it's a lovely starry, moonlit night there is nothing more beautiful. We take a bottle of pop and some smoked salmon sandwiches and sit on the edge of the moor to watch what everyone else is doing in the village. We have our little 'Peace' up there and we take whatever animals we've got, the pet lambs, the cat, everything than can come with us does.

Mary Bailey

Miss Hodgkinson's legacy lives on in the conveyance of Carhead Moor, which she donated to the National Park authority in 1978, in that the moor remains wild – in accordance with her wish 'not to permit or suffer any sheep to be grazed on the said land'.

LIFE ON THE FARM

Talk to anyone about North Lees Hall or Farm and two names will crop up time and time again. The Ollerenshaw and Prigent families lived and farmed at North Lees Farm for over one-hundred-and-fifty years. Not only are they respected but they are also held in great affection by people from all parts of the community.

In June 1977, Jabez Ollerenshaw, at the age of 91 years, and his brother, Arthur, were interviewed for Radio Sheffield. If anyone knew what life on the farm was about, these two did, painting word pictures of a way of life that has gone forever. Jabez tells his story –

One of the most wonderful things that I've ever come across in my life was the self-binder to tie the corn up.

It cut and sheaved and tied up the corn. The horses pulled the share round the field and threw it out to the side so there was room for them to come round again. I don't know how they'd manage today growing corn as it used to be in our day. We had to do so much by hand when I was a lad. I used to do work which even a man wouldn't do today because I was brought up to it and it wasn't no hardship to me.

Back then it didn't matter if a job had to be done at night, a turn in the weather; we had to do it. I remember one occasion; I was only quite a little lad, before I started school. We'd some hay nearly dry and the farmer had been up and looked at the weatherglass and he realised it was going to rain. So he fetched me out of bed before it was light and I had to get on the cart and load a load of hay with him throwing it up to me. And I was only half-awake and I didn't feel safe at all but I'd got to do it. I don't think I'd have been more than five or six.

Before we started school we'd got work to do in the morning, looking after horses and suckling cows. I used to turn the horses out, feed them and clean them out and give them hay. Sometimes I had to do the milking of a morning as well. We had to be at school for nine o'clock so we had to be off from North Lees by half-past-eight. There was none of this being taken to school in those days; we had to walk there and back again. Mother packed up dinner and I used to carry it in a special bag over my shoulder.

There was me, my brother Arthur and my two sisters and we got to a point where I thought that my brother ought to take some responsibility about it. One day I told him I wasn't going to bring the bag back. If I took it full he'd have to bring it back empty. He wasn't going to do that so the bag got left at school. When I got near home I started thinking and I realised what my mother'd say if there was no bag to take the meal next morning. At the last minute I decided I'd have to go back again although I'd had nothing but the bit of breakfast in the early morning and the packed lunch and I was pretty hungry. Back I went to Hathersage School and brought the bag ready for next morning.

Very often we'd take bread and dripping, bread and butter, sometimes bread and treacle and sometimes, very rare, we had meat. Not because we couldn't have it if we wanted it but because we never fancied it. Mother baked all the bread at home. You used to get flour in ten stone bags and we had our own oatmeal, which we'd grown and had milled, at Broughton Mill. But we were always encouraged to eat as much of that as we wanted because it didn't cost us much.

One incident that happened when I was a youngster at North Lees Hall was just after we started school; my brother and I started together. I didn't start school till I was eight, or seven anyway, because I didn't have anyone to go with and our people wouldn't let us go alone.

It had been snowing all morning and there was quite thick snow on the ground. Father and mother wouldn't let any of us go to school. It cleared up at dinnertime and the sun came out and my mother had no barm so she packed me off to Hathersage for some barm and gave me some money for it. I couldn't go over the shorter way because there was no track at all so I had to go the long way round, past Coachman's Cottage for Brookfield Manor.

There'd be about three or four inches of snow, which made it heavy walking. As I was going past Mrs Hill came out and says 'Are you going to the village?'

I says 'Yes' and she says 'Will you bring me some yeast?'

'Well, I'd no idea what yeast was and I didn't like to tell her I didn't know so I thought if I say it's yeast when I get to the shop they'll probably know what I mean. Anyway when I got near to the village I met some of my school pals and I couldn't remember east, west, north nor south. So I got my mother's things and Mrs Hill'd given me some money for barm and a penny for myself. I couldn't help but spend this penny, I bought a spice pig. I thought, 'Well, I'll take it back and give it her'.

Anyway I couldn't resist eating it. When I got back to the cottage and was going past the door she came out and says 'Here, have you brought my yeast?'

I says 'No.'

She says 'Why haven't you?'

'I couldn't remember.'

'What have you bought for your mother?'

'Some barm.'

'Well, you Johnny, that's what I wanted.'

'Well, you didn't tell me so.'

'Give me that money back and my penny.'

I said 'I can't.'

She says 'Why can't you?'

I said 'I bought a spice pig.'

'Well, give me that – that'll do five children.'

'I've eaten it,' I said.

Years and years later I recorded this on paper and sent it to a competition at the Hope Valley College Golden Age Group and won a prize with it.

The area's famous for the Bronte connection and I knew an old couple, Mr and Mrs Thorpe, that lived at Sandylee Cottage, who could remember Charlotte Bronte coming to stay at North Lees whilst she was writing the story of Jane Eyre. She took the name from the Eyre family who'd lived at North Lees and used Geer Green School as the place that Jane Eyre taught.

When I grew up and left home I went to a local farm where I used to carry milk into Hathersage in two or three gallon churns with a yoke on my back. I delivered it in open cans, door to door. It was tuppence-half-penny a pint.

We moved to Riley when I got married. We'd had no telephone and no tap either. All the water was pumped out of a well thirty feet below us. Every drop of water, for heating and washing and providing food, feeding cows and pigs and animals and cleaning vessels, milk vessels and everything, all had to be pumped and all the heating had to be done in the side boiler or in a pan and kettles.

We always had to have a fire, every day, no matter how hot it was, to cook our meals. Now we can even have a cup of tea in our bedroom. Never thought about that when I was a child. We never thought that was a possibility. That's how much things have changed.

Jabez Ollerenshaw

Arthur picks up the story –

My father was a farmer and when I left school I had to go into farming. I had no choice whatever but I think farming life was what I'd have chosen for myself.

There weren't that many choices for anyone. One of the main industries in those days was the pin industry. There were three or four different mills in the village where they turned out pins. I suppose they were used for combing out wool. There were stone masons – they used to get the stone out of Millstone Edge, you know, to build houses down in the village here and there's quite a lot of them lost their lives through the stone dust getting onto their lungs. They died at an early age, about forty and fifty; a lot of them up in the churchyard only lived half a life.

There was nothing else. When the railway was made, the Dore and Chinley line, which I can just remember, it brought work. I think it opened in 1893.

I remember them making the levels from the hills and that kind of thing. I know when the railway was completed the railway company gave a free ride up to Edale to all the school children. My brother and I were only very young then and our parents wouldn't let us go on such a long distance as that. It was a big treat in those days.

I went to school in Hathersage. I used to do all sorts of daft things, like any other lad, and I don't suppose they're much different today – although we hadn't the time on our hands. We were always found plenty of work and we had to do it too. No question of being out of work in those days. You had to work for a living otherwise you got to starve or go into the workhouse

I enjoyed school in one way and in another way I didn't. I'd rather be at home or outside. There was a very strict schoolmaster in my younger days. It wasn't a case of sparing the rod and spoiling the child – we got plenty of cane. Used to use that pretty heavily sometimes. Mind you, I resented it at the time but it didn't do me any harm at all.

We played truant occasionally, perhaps catching trout down in the local brooks. Sometimes we'd go and rob somebody's garden of apples. Then we'd face the music when we got back to school but only if we were caught. We weren't always caught!

We didn't do it that often. The truant officer was in Bakewell and if you were away too often he'd come out and you had to explain why you were away. That happened once or twice.

When things started to change, when more visitors came to the village, I think we rather welcomed it. When I was about nine or ten years old Dad used to go to Sheffield and take all the produce and sell it. I used to go down with him sometimes on the horse and spring-cart. That took us about an hour to an hour-and-a-half from North Lees to Sheffield.

One Saturday morning we were going down High Street and in front of us I could see a group of people gathered together looking at something. We didn't know what it was until we got to it and found out it was one of the first motor cars that came into Sheffield.

It was a good few years before cars came to our area. I remember the first one coming into this district. When I was about sixteen years old I worked in the garden at Brookfield Manor. This was when the Cammels were in residence. They'd got a chauffeur from London because there weren't any around here. Between Brookfield Manor and Hathersage there were four gates to open. It was my job to open and close these gates after

Arthur and Ray Ollerenshaw at Swaledale Sheep Sales
© The Prigent/Ollerenshaw families

the chauffeur had driven through.

One day we were going down the drive and the chauffeur said to me 'We're going to try this car out and see what mileage it actually will do.' He put his foot down on the accelerator and pulled all the stops out and we were going. We got halfway down the drive and he called out to me 'We're doing thirty!' That was some speed then.

Later on, when I was farming, I didn't have very much leisure time. I never did any cricketing or football or anything like that. I'd no time; it was all taken up on the farm.

In summer time I used to get up at four o'clock in the morning for getting the horses in and feeding them. Then I'd go mowing while the weather was cool. When I'd mowed a couple or three acres I'd take the horses in, feed them, feed myself then after we'd had breakfast get out in the field again to turn the crop over. We used to shake it out by hand with forks and as the day went on, when perhaps the hay had dried, we'd get it into rows, long rows, by hand, all by hand of course. When it was hay-time we worked all the while it was daylight. We wouldn't be finished till ten o'clock.

It's a bit different today. Farming's quite different altogether. They don't know what work is on farms today. They won't work unless there's a seat on it. Got to have a seat on it to make the thing go. It was all hand work in my time. Hard work, too.

Mind you things are produced very much better. Bigger crops because they've fertilised the land to such an extent now that you get twice as much crop off the same acreage.

I'd never done any mole catching, not when I was farming. No time to catch moles then but when I retired some of the farmers said 'Can you catch us some of the moles?' I said 'I'll do me best,' got some traps and got interested in it and well, I don't know, I think I've cleared most of the moles round the immediate district.

I've got a special trap, a spring trap. You simply find out where the moles are working, you can see where the moles are working, and find the main run. Usually on a farm it'll be in a wall-side or a hedge-bottom. I had a special trap, a spring trap, and you put your trap in the main run and set

it. I've caught as many as, well, in the teens in one trap in one season.
And I'm still catching them now.

Arthur Ollerenshaw

But changes didn't stop with the turn of the century. The late Eric Ollerenshaw, brother to Muriel Prigent, wrote the following memories of childhood at North Lees Farm for publication in Hathersage Remembers, published by the Hathersage Millennium Group.

One of my first memories was of a German Zeppelin flying over Hathersage at the end of the First World War and my father rushing in from the farm buildings on the edge of darkness shouting, 'Put that light out.' We had a small paraffin lamp with a wick burner. We put out the light immediately and waited for the zoom of the Zeppelin to die away.

North Lees is the house in which I was born and lived for twenty-seven years. There was a notice pinned behind the front door which read: 'Tenants will be allowed to charge visitors 3d each to show them round the house', which could be done in approximately twenty minutes.

I can still smell the soap suds as they filled the old farm kitchen every Monday morning. A large room with stone flags on the floor, a stone sink with only cold water on tap, a Yorkshire range with side boiler which leaked smoke in at the top so that we had to skim off the soot to use the water. A primitive 'copper', which held about eight gallons of water, was heated by a coal fire. Wash day would be all day for nine children and two adults; my mother only had a 'peggy tub'. Wednesday was baking day – twenty-four full size loaves, two ovens full. Thursday was churning and butter making. We often churned for two hours before the cream turned to butter. I have known times when we had to sell all our butter to buy margarine, we were so poor. Even so the days of my childhood were very happy days and my mum had a wonderful trust in God, otherwise she would not have survived the awful struggle of bringing up nine children.

I started school at five-and-a-half years and had to be at the next farm by 7.45am to travel with Eddy in the milk float for the last mile. Eddy used to sing 'Swanee River' at the top of his voice as we jogged into Hathersage. But coming home was different. I could not find my way and got lost many times. My mum would find me at the end of a path leading to nowhere, crying my eyes out, and not until I was eight-and-a-half did they discover that my sight was so poor I could not see my way. I was then taken to the 'clinic', which was in Chinley, to have a sight test. One eye was blind and the other eye very short sighted. I was prescribed a pair of glasses and in eighteen months had learned to read and write and find my way about.

As a boy on the farm I had each week to walk to the next farm, Birley Farm, about a mile away, to collect the weekly supply of eggs. Sometimes they were still in the nesting boxes from the whole week and were very grubby and needed cleaning before my father could take them to Sheffield with his own produce for sale. He travelled every Friday by Burbage and Ringinglow which was in those days a rough cart-track with rocks and boulders to negotiate. Travelling with him one day in the trap he remarked that 'One day I wouldn't be surprised if this is tarmaced, but not in our time.'

Eric Ollerenshaw

The more recent farmers, Cecil and Muriel Prigent, nee Ollerenshaw, with their children, experienced the good and the bad of hill farming life and can chronicle the changes that have taken place in the area since Muriel's childhood when she and her six brothers and two sisters had the North Lees Estate as a back-drop to their lives. Muriel's memories of life at North Lees go back to the nineteen-twenties.

Four generations of us have lived at North Lees. Granddad Ollerenshaw first, then my dad with his brothers and sisters, then us and then our own children. It never belonged to us, we only rented it from General Beech.

When I was born the Hall was in ruins. We lived in the farmhouse part and were still there when they restored the Hall in 1964. That was when we first got an inside toilet. Before that we used to have to go out across the back yard, up the steps and round to the pig cotes. We had to keep the door shut in case there were any rats about. It was horrible.

Mum had eleven children but she lost two, one in childbirth and the other, who had a bad heart, died when he was six weeks old.

There was a seventeen year spread over all of the children. I was in the middle, my oldest brother was seven years older than me and Lois, the youngest, was ten years younger than me.

There was no nurse or doctor to deliver babies then. The neighbours used to come and everybody knew what they were doing. It's amazing when you think about it.

Of course, mothers never dreamt of going out to work in those days. They stayed at home and looked after their family. They worked very hard in comparison to nowadays. The stone floors, not the easiest of things to keep clean, are all back in fashion. I never thought I'd see that.

Waking up with no central heating and having to scrape the ice off the inside of the bedroom window and having to get dressed under the bed-clothes. Those lovely patterns you used to get on the inside of the curtains and things. And having to light the fire before you could have any heat.

My dad was always up first. He'd light the fire and put this great big iron kettle on. It was huge but with all of us there it had to be a big one. And then Mum cooked breakfast for all of us.

Our water came down from Stanage. It just ran overground. Sheila remembers getting worms and tadpoles and all sorts of fish in it. We used to have a little net underneath the tap because we used to get all sorts of bugs.

My mother used to walk down to the village with various children in the pram, on the pram and hanging onto it. She'd do the shopping then push it all the way back again. That was about a two miles walk back home on a very steep, very rough bit of cart track. One day the bull came for us when she'd got two of us in the pram. Fortunately my Dad was looking out for her and managed to get the bull off while my mother pulled the pram. The bulls were left with the cows and Dad had just forgotten that he was in the field.

Every Friday we'd take the pony and trap to Sheffield market. We took butter, eggs, cream and potatoes to sell and brought all our groceries back.

My dad used to walk tups from Kirby Stevens and buy up some sheep and walk them back. He stayed at farms on the way and left a sheep for his keep for the night. That'd take him about a week.

When it was shearing time all the neighbours and friends used to come to help. They'd bring their wives and children and we'd have about thirty sat around the kitchen table for lunch and tea.

There was an old tramp called Gee who loved to buy white calves. I don't know what he did with them, but he only wanted white ones. He used to stay a bit in the barn and we gave him sandwiches and that sort of thing. Then he'd move on and come back perhaps in say a year's time and he'd take a calf with him. Yes, a white one. I don't know how he transported them. Perhaps he put a bit of string around their necks or something.

He came for lots of years, he was always on the road. He went where he knew people would give him food. I suppose he lived in people's barns and so on.

Then there was Jack Putty. Jack was the man who used to replace windows and if he had not got any business he'd go out at night and break people's windows, so that they'd ring him up and give him the work.

When we got home from school at night we all had our jobs to do before we could go and play; get the sticks in for lighting the fire the next morning, that sort of thing. We had an old crosscut saw we used to saw logs. No electric saws then. The cinders had to be riddled, the coal to be got in, the calves to be suckled at night when we got home. But we had plenty of time to play.

We didn't help with the washing but my mother used to be still washing when we got home at five o'clock at night and she'd started at five o'clock in the morning when she put the copper on. Her fingers were all rough where she'd been rubbing the socks.

The copper was in a corner of the huge kitchen. There used to be the copper in the corner and next to it there was a bakestone where they made the oat cakes.So it was cold meat and wet washing on a Monday.

When it was wet or snowing we had a huge clothes-horse we used to stand up and drape the clothes over it. We had a pully eventually but not when I was small.

There was a fireguard around a big fire and then the clothes-horse went in front of that. We didn't wear so many clothes as they do today, we didn't change them as often as we do today.

I remember the days before wellingtons when we wore little leather button boots that we used to walk to school in. I've still got my little button hook that I used to button my boots up with. They kept the wet out because we put dubbin on them to waterproof them. Not that it was done every day, not with nine of us.

But we never suffered with anything. None of us had rheumatism. We used to sit in wet clothes sometimes all day at school, having to walk to school. I don't think any of us have had any rheumatism or anything.

We used to bait the horses; about five o'clock in the morning we used to get up and feed the horses, that's what 'bait' means.

My dad was the pig-killer for all around and about and the boys used to blow the bladder up and use it as a football. It was a cheap toy, something to do. He didn't get bacon in exchange for killing them. They used to pay him so much a pig.

There was a big beam in the farmhouse kitchen and in the winter time all the beams were hung with sides of bacons and hams. I can picture them now. Every morning before we went to school mother would slice off some bacon, put the kettle on and cook us bacon and eggs. We dipped our bread in the bacon fat. It was lovely.

They say 'don't eat this, don't eat that' but you have to remember we used to walk everywhere. Two miles to school – we needed good food.

The Headmaster at the school was a really old-fashioned, funny little chap. His daughter, Nora Roden, was the infant teacher. He was a nice man, I don't remember him using the cane.

My four brothers were older than me so, of course, when I left school I stayed home and helped mother to do all the work. Mixing the bread, two stones of flour at a time. That made just over a dozen loaves. We did that twice a week. Just for our family.

When you think about how people did their housework then! It was amazing.

It's no wonder they didn't go out to do any other work, they didn't have time. They must have been made of very good stuff.

And we're long-livers. My mother was ninety-five and my dad was ninety-seven when they died, so it must have been a healthy life up there.

And I'm eight-one but I still cook for about forty-four on a Monday. There's four of us that cook for the old folks.

Growing up at North Lees – it was wonderful, it really was. There were nine of us so we were very self-contained. We had our family and we didn't really need anyone from outside. We had our own football and cricket teams.

It was idyllic. It really was.

My husband was a soldier in the Army. He was stationed at Hathersage – they had soldiers at the Memorial Hall and at the Institute at the bottom of the village. He came from the Channel Isles, hence the French name. His mother and younger brothers and sisters were evacuated to Brighouse in Yorkshire but his grandparents stayed on and died from malnutrition during the war.

His family went back to Guernsey but he never did, not to stay.

I met him when I was nineteen. He was in the regular army before the war started so he was one of the first to go to France but he wasn't there long because he wasn't old enough to be there. When his mother found out he'd gone she wrote to the officials and got him back. He wasn't very pleased with her for that!

He was discharged as medically unfit because of an injury and he came back here but for most of his army life after that he was fire-fighting in London.

I'd worked on the farm until a year before we were married. Then I told my mother I wanted to get a bit of money ready to buy things for the house that we'd have when we were married. Mum said yes because I was the oldest girl and I had stayed at home but never got any wages. I just did the work and that was that. If I wanted anything I asked my dad and depending on whether he was flush or not I'd sometimes get it, sometimes not. I was quite happy living like that until I needed to save up.

They'd just started an ammunitions place at the bottom of the village and I went there. The munitions place was at the Institute and I made twist drills.

Most of the village girls went there. They'd been in service before that.

When my husband was first demobbed he came to meet me at the gate as I came out of work. He was wearing his de-mob suit that was miles to big for him. Most men hated them, absolutely loathed them!

We married in 1942, right bang in the middle of the war. Everything was rationed but they managed to put on a proper spread at the George Hotel.

I had to have coupons for my wedding dress. It was nothing spectacular but it was a white one.

We went to live in Brighouse for about five years. And the two older children were born there. I hated it. It's a big town, about the size of Bakewell, and that's big after North Lees. I needed to get back here.

None of my brothers wanted to take the farm over at North Lees and it was suggested to us that we came back and run it. Of course we jumped at it – well, I jumped at it!

My husband was quite happy but no one in his family had ever farmed. He had a lot of learning to do. My younger brother stayed with us. He wasn't married at that point and he was farming at North Lees, so he stayed with us for a couple of years before he went out to Kenya.

We had a search light battery on our land, at the top of the wood where the warden's place is. The search lights were left on at night, looking for bombers coming over. They were heading for the steelworks at Sheffield.

And there were mock-ups on the moors, just to put them off the scent. If they'd got their markers out it only took a bit of wind to blow them off course and they'd bomb somewhere else. My eldest brother, Eric, had a poultry farm and he found an incendiary under one of the hen-cotes. It hadn't gone off and he called in the bomb disposal unit.

A gentleman tells the story of going out over Stanage with a School Scout Troop. They'd got their route planned out and walked over from Sheffield. When they got to the Prisoner-of-War Camp at Redmires someone warned them to be careful because some prisoners were lost. They spotted some smoke coming out of a cave so they got down really low and peered in and it was the prisoners. They were wearing brown overalls with great big yellow spots on, about a foot wide. Two of the Scouts stayed and kept watch and they really didn't know what they'd do if the prisoners came out. The other two Scouts ran all the way to Hathersage to get the police and the army. The funniest bit is that the prisoners were just so relieved to be found. It was freezing cold and they'd spent two nights in the cave. All they could think was 'Take me back'! It was a wonderful adventure for the Scouts, absolutely great, and the prisoners, who were Italians, were really friendly.

It was lovely to walk on Stanage Edge and go into Robin Hood's Cave. There were porridge bowls there, that's what they said when we were kids. They are stones which have been hewn out to make deep bowls that the birds used as water bowls.

Little John's grave is in the churchyard at Hathersage. The Cave was a hideout and Little John is supposed to have sent an arrow from there into the churchyard and that's how he comes to be buried there.

I lived at North Lees for 64 years of my life. I often say I've been very blessed with a wonderful life. It's not everybody that can say that, can they?

Muriel Prigent

The next generation on from Muriel and her brothers and sisters saw tremendous changes that affected everyones lives but living on a hill farm still presented its challenges. Sheila tells her story ....

I was born in 1955 so I'm the baby of the family.

It was lovely growing up at North Lees, I loved the open space. We'd just go off and get lost. It was wonderful. Even when my two were little they'd wander off with a packet of sandwiches and a bottle of pop and I could just let them go.

Robin Hood's Cave was a great place to play. My mum played up there, so did I and so did my children.

You have to actually climb down into the cave, you can't see it from the top unless you know where it is.

We didn't spend nights up there but we knew some boys that did. One of them fell out onto the rocks below. It's just below Stanage Edge so it's quite high up. Years ago Sheffield kids used to come and sleep there nearly every weekend. I'm not sure how they managed it because there were rats and all sorts in there.

We used to keep the cade lambs, the ones who had either lost their mother or had been rejected, in the garden. We bottle-feed them and gave them a name – then we ate them! People would say 'What happens to them when they've grown up? Did you say they go in the deep-freeze? Oh, you couldn't do that.' But there was no compunction about that because that's what they were there for.

It's very difficult for people to understand that you can rear animals and look after them, care for them, be concerned for them, but still know that they're going to be eaten. Our animals were important to us, we wouldn't have wanted to see them hurt or injured in any way, but we still had in the back of our minds that they were reared for food. That makes you view human life differently as well, with the cycle of the seasons and so on.

I helped kill them, slit their throats. It's not allowed now but there's a lot coming out about how much better it is for the animals to be slaughtered at home. Far less stressful, none of this being taken abroad and getting scared.

I wouldn't let my own children do it because they haven't grown up with it.

My brother's wife has got a different outlook on things. She finds it difficult to understand this natural acceptance that we are rearing the animals to eat them. It was a natural progression that you reared your own and you killed your own. It was the norm.

I went to the school in Hathersage, the same one that my mum and my granddad went to and it's still a school now.

When the weather was really bad we'd have the day off because the taxi couldn't get to pick us up but if it started snowing when we were in school, all those living on the outlying farms would say 'Dad'll be coming to fetch us soon in case we get snowed in.'

By the time we were going to school cooked breakfasts were a thing of the past. We didn't have time to eat bacon and eggs. We were more into cereals and dripping and Bovril. Toast and dripping. Lovely.

We had our own Guernsey cow so we had milk from her. We'd go and milk her by hand and drink it straight from her. We didn't boil it or anything.

We had campers on our land and some teenage lads came asking if they could have a pint of milk. We said 'Well, Dad's just up in the yard milking the cow. If you want to go and wait for him to finish you can have your milk.'

They stood in the doorway and watched my dad and one of them said 'Here Mister, our milk doesn't come from there, it comes in bottles.'

He was being deadly serious. He'd no idea where it came from.

And we collected eggs from hens when they were still warm and they were nothing like the ones that you buy in the shops.

Hill farmers are a dying breed now because things have changed so much. In a lot of instances it's cheaper to import food than it is to produce it here so the financial side is difficult too. Coming from a farming family I think it's disgraceful that food is imported and our home produced food isn't used.

One of the problems is that the industry here has such high standards that our farmers have to work to but they don't have those standards on the Continent. They're supposed to but they just get away with it. That means they can produce it cheaper than we can in this country.

Hathersage used to be a village for farmers but now the farms have gone and tourism has taken over. There's a lot of commuters living there, too. That has the effect of pricing the houses out of the reach of local youngsters who've grown up here. It's one of the downsides to living in the Peak District; it carries a price tag.

Now the village has three shops for climbers and walkers. When I go into them I think about my dad. He thought there should be an open season on shooting tourists! He prayed for rain every Bank Holiday. Most farmers did.

One of the problems was the crowds of visitors walking through the crops. They didn't understand country life. One Sunday afternoon he found a party of people having a picnic in the hayfield. When he told them it was private land and they shouldn't be there they said 'Oh, it's the National Park, we can go where we want.'

At lambing time people would find a lamb, tuck it under their arm and bring it down to the house saying 'It's abandoned.'

Mum would just say 'Take it back where you got it from, the mother won't be far away.'

Dogs used to be let off leads and would get the sheep worried.

When the Peak Park was formed Tom Tomlinson, who was the first Warden, and my Dad worked on opening up the moor at Stanage. Tom used to take parties of school children round and they worshiped the ground he walked on.

Tom and Dad did the Warden's job between them. Dad was an unofficial Warden, he didn't get paid for it. Their job was to encourage walkers and climbers but to make sure the visitors knew how to behave in the countryside.

We used to make a bit of money out of them, selling orange juice on Sundays at the top of the wood. Sixpence a glass or whatever! We wished they'd all go home and leave us alone but at the same time we were making money out of them.

Even when the weather's really bad you still get people coming out to climb or walk. They endanger their lives. We didn't have a Mountain Rescue team so it was the Wardens who used to bring people down who'd fallen off the rocks. We had a Wardens sledge with a stretcher on that was kept in the farm buildings. They had a room in the barn to start with and the first aid equipment was stored at the farm.

When they started rock-climbing they came with ropes and just climbed. They didn't have helmets or proper shoes. What they had were their mother's washing lines. It was certainly a lot more casual when it first started, people used to come and just scramble up the rocks.

In fact, some of the girls wore bikinis to climb and they had to be fetched down because the rocks were hot and touching them with bare skin made them jerk away and fall off.

Joe Brown used to come out quite a lot and Sir Edmund Hillary came for a cup of tea one day.

It started off as working class thing in the early 1900's. Now it's all types of people that get involved. People have more leisure time and want to do these things.

Of course when the hang-gliders started, we had one who came down at the edge of the rocks with his head straight between two rocks. My dad went up in the Landrover to let him down.

There were crowds of people that used to walk over from Sheffield, over the top of Stanage down into Hathersage but you'd never see any walkers walking that sort of distance now. They all bring their cars up to Stanage Edge.

When I was a young girl there were more flowers around, probably because we didn't use fertilisers. We just put cow-muck back onto the fields.

We were organic before it became fashionable.

The rise of tourism has meant that wildlife has paid a price. Our cousin farms up there – he was saying that when the moors were closed last year, because of foot and mouth, how much more wildlife and bird life there was on the moors. And he said he noticed how quickly they went again when they opened the moors.

It's difficult because the people that come to the moors enjoy the wildlife and, through no fault of their own, the wildlife are leaving the area. There's concern at the moment about the ring ouzels not being there. They're a bit like blackbirds. Ring ouzels are quite rare and climbers are disturbing them so there are areas that are voluntary no-climbing areas. If they can keep people away from them they'll have a chance to breed.

But there are still people who go bird-nesting and take the eggs. People are more aware but there are still some who do it. Birds of prey eggs are more at risk because they fetch big money. Something like a goshawk is worth thousands and thousands of pounds.

We often saw kingfishers under one particular bridge but we never see them now. The hares and stoats are still around and there are badgers in

THE OLLERENSHAW AND PRIGENT FAMILY TREE

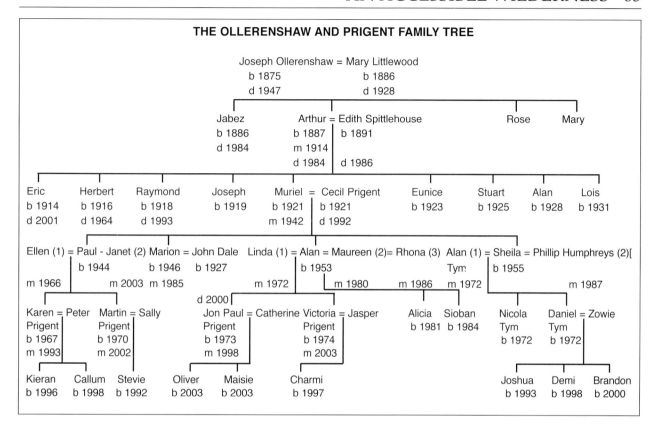

Left:
Arthur and Ethel Ollerenshaw
© Muriel Prigent

Right:
Muriel and Cecil Prigent
© Muriel Prigent

Left:
Paul Prigent, Marion Dale (nee Prigent), Alan Prigent and Sheila Humphreys (nee Prigent)
© Sheila Humphreys

Right:
Muriel and Cecil Prigent at North Lees Hall Farm
© Muriel Prigent

Birley woods. People don't realise how big and strong they are. If they come to a fence they'll push at it and push at it until they get through. We used to just accept they were on our land and that was fine until we found a lamb that had been killed. It wasn't a fox, you can tell when it is because he pulls the throat out. A badger just bites at them all over. Foxes just kill for the sake of killing. Like they do with hens, they just kill the lot and don't bother eating any of them.

I don't think I realised when I was growing up just how beautiful it was. When you grow up in that environment you just take it for granted.

It is beautiful – there's no doubt about it. It's the beauty and the isolation.

I'd go back if I could. After all that space. I still have trouble coping with neighbours, even though I've been in the village for sixteen years.

I'd love to go back.

Sheila Humphreys

It takes a dream and a dreamer to take on the type of project that was North Lees Hall.

By 1959 the Hall was derelict; few of the magnificent interior features remained apart from the spiral staircase and the three-foot wide walls. Not a lot to base a restoration project on but sufficient for Lieutenant-Colonel Gerald Haythornthwaite to imagine the Hall restored to its former glory.

As an architect he was not only able to visualise the restoration but brought architectural skills to show how it could be achieved.

But restoration is a costly business. The owner, Lieutenant-Colonel Beach, took on most of the financial burden in memory of his parents, Major-General 'Bill' Beach and Constance Maud (nee Cammell).

Further substantial help was given by The Ministry of Public Buildings and Works, who gave a grant for the most urgent of the necessary repairs and Gerald Haythornthwaite saw his dream become reality.

When the work was complete the Hall, like many other farms in the area, diversified. Muriel and Cecil Prigent ran bed-and-breakfast. Around this time Lieutenant-Colonel Beach approached the Peak Park Joint Planning Board with a view to selling them the estate. As public money had been used for part of the restoration one of the conditions of sale was that the Hall should be opened for the benefit of the public. Today people from all walks of life are able to enjoy the splendour of the building.

Many people dream of working in the countryside. Robert Helliwell made that dream into reality.

I was born in Baulk Lane, in Hathersage then was lucky enough to live at North Lees where I worked as the Manager of Broomfield College. I worked there for thirteen years and lived there for two.

It was a funny place to live because you couldn't get your stuff up there, you couldn't get the car up. We had to park the car right down the track and walk it.

On good days, when it was quiet, it was a lovely place to live but at weekends you got lots of people walking past. Occasionally they'd get in the way of the livestock but it wasn't too bad. The majority of them were fairly keen to know what we were doing but would keep out of the way.

The farm was taken over when the Prigents left. They used to keep poultry there. There was a lot to do. It was in a run down state, walls were down and the sheep that were there were of poor quality, so it was a case of upgrade everything really. That was my job.

The Hall wasn't taken over at that point. We lived in the service wing. The back door was open in the Hall and sheep used to wander in and out. The ground floor was in a bit of a state. It was a nice shelter for them!

There wasn't much help but I was able to employ a shepherd. That was all on the farming side.

I saw a lot of changes whilst I was up at the Farm. The biggest, I suppose, was over the last couple of years with problems with foot and mouth. That brought incomes down to rock-bottom.

What was a reasonable holding which would have looked after a family is now no longer viable. Farmers have to increase the numbers of sheep and take more acres as they become available so the small farm is disappearing.

I should think you could survive if you had something like six or seven hundred sheep but a farmer would really want to be looking at a few more than that. It all depends on world market prices. We're very much affected by what's happening in the world, rather than just in Hathersage and Derbyshire and England now – it's much more broad-based.

The business of buying in cheaper meat from the Continent, South America, Africa and places like that has really hit the people badly around here. It has had an effect.

A lot of the farms in the area tend to be family farms and as such they tend to hang on as long as possible. They might even own their own farm, therefore they haven't got rent to pay, so that makes life a bit easier. It's still eating into their capital, which they've possibly put away for when they retire. There's a farm in the village – the last dairy farm in the village – where there are three sons. Two of them now work away from home. One of them works on the farm but he does contract work and that's with a dairy-herd of three hundred and fifty cows and they can't keep going. What they really need is more money from the milking side. So they've changed direction; the two sons have gone out to work and it's unlikely that they'll come back, and they've also put up the buildings and converted others, more traditional ones, to bunkhouses. That's cushioning the farm.

So there are farms that have disappeared and the house has been sold for a tremendous amount of money, maybe half a million, for a house which would have been the hub of a small farm. And they're going to commuters and ones that can afford it. That changes the life of the area.

The larger numbers of visitors have changed it too. There's an increase in the amount of walkers but I think there's a bigger increase in climbers, hang-gliders and all that.

More spare time means an increase in visitors and that puts a lot more pressure on Stanage.

People return to Stanage time and time again. The climbing is easy because Stanage has got loads of different climbs, different degrees of difficulty and it's fairly accessible. You've only got a short walk from the

Sheep and lambs
© Robert Helliwell

Para-glider over Stanage
© Peak District National Park Authority

road and it's up the hill. A short walk and you're there.

People come back because of the views and the scenery and for this thing called 'wildness'; the remoteness of it and the tranquillity. Sadly, the fact that so many people come back for that is actually removing it. They are destroying the very thing they come for. It's very difficult to explain to people.

We watch out for wild flowers but, again, if you advertise it you'll tend to lose them. It's the same with wildlife. We look for it on Stanage and the moorland around it but if we increase the number of visitors that go up there, we'll lose it all. Somewhere along the line we have to ask 'do we have to have an area as a sacrifice?' 'Can Stanage be a sacrifice area because it's so accessible?'

I get the impression that's what's happening now.

One thing I was going to mention about visitors is North Lees Hall and the Bronte connection. There are an awful lot of visitors who just came to walk past and look at it and photograph it. There are a lot of Americans, a lot of Japanese, who are after this connection with Bronte. I used to take school parties around North Lees. If you mention the connection to English children they don't know who Charlotte Bronte was yet the children who visited from the Czech Republic knew all about her.

I can see some merit in trying to limit the numbers of people that come, but I can also see that if you do that you will create an area that is either for those people that can afford to live there – in other words those people with lots of money – or we'll end up at the opposite end of the spectrum; people who survive there, on low income, because they're perhaps in farming or a rural occupation. The cost of living is quite high; the cost of Council Tax is high, the cost of housing is high. It's just an expensive area to live in.

The numbers of visitors is a perennial problem but there is no easy answer. One half of you says yes to the visitors, bringing with them a healthier economy, the other half says no, they spoil the place. But then again, you could argue that it isn't right for us to have the place to ourselves. It's very difficult. There is no easy answer.

Robert Helliwell

LIFE ON THE EDGE

The Peak District National Park was created in 1951, the very first National Park in the United Kingdom. A lot of people thought it was a ridiculous idea to have it here because of all the industry. Why not, for instance, have it in Northern Scotland? Bill Darley has reason to celebrate its creation as he became one of the first Rangers who shaped the new Park.

People thought it wasn't going to work at all. There were no other Ranger Services in the country so there was no experience to go on and it was the first time that any National Park Authority had negotiated access to the moors, so it was working from absolute scratch.

To begin with they had one full-time Ranger, Tom Tomlinson, and it wasn't until 1959, when it was decided that the Peak Park would negotiate access agreements for ramblers, that a team of Rangers was employed. It was now possible for the National Park Authority to acquire land that had not previously been available but, in return for that, landowners wanted a form of policing. They wanted to make sure access agreements and by-laws were kept. The first access agreement was at Kinder Scout, the site of the 1932 Trespass.

They needed to get a team together to start the first patrol in Edale. There were four of us, Wardens rather than Rangers, all chosen for different reasons. For years a group of us had a cottage in Edale and we used to go out every weekend, so we knew the area and a lot of the local people. I was a walker and did a lot of climbing and mountaineering and I think those were the reasons I was chosen.

One of the others was chosen because he was a school-teacher in Rotherham. It was thought that anybody connected with education would be an asset. Another was chosen because he was in the legal profession and the fourth was a leading member in the Ramblers Association.

We had no equipment or anything. In those days Fred Heardman was the landlord at the Nag's Head. He was a member of the Planning Board but was very pro national parks. He allowed us to use one of his rooms as a briefing centre so the very first meeting of the Peak District National Park Wardens started. Nobody had any idea what was going to happen.

The first Sunday we set up and had a briefing at ten o'clock. Fred opened the door and there was a queue of people that stretched a considerable way down the main street in Edale. They were mainly members of walking clubs who were very keen because they'd got access at last onto Kinder Scout. That caused us our first problem. The bigger rambling clubs were probably thirty or forty people strong. How do you send thirty or forty people with one Assistant Warden on to Kinder? The idea was that we would explain where they could go and then at various times we'd meet up with them and see how they were getting on, and it worked. Everybody was so enthusiastic.

We carried on like that for about two years but we realised it was hopeless having these big concentrations of people. You never really knew who would turn up so they employed Wardens on a part-time basis. That way you knew they would be there, they were paid staff. And that's the way the Ranger Service works today.

We had an access agreement on the eastern side of Kinder, which was Glossop and Hayfield, and we operated from there and Hayfield. Shortly after that we got an access agreement on Stanage.

In those days Stanage was owned by Colonel Beach. I never met him, I don't think anybody ever did because he was a serving officer in the Army. Possibly his Land Agent thought it sounded a good idea to have an access agreement because he knew there'd be people looking after the area because as far as I knew they didn't employ a Game-keeper. I found out later that, in fact, they did. Some of the Gamekeepers in other areas were a bit anti the plans.

Up to that point nobody had been able to go to those places, at least not officially. That isn't to say people didn't walk on Kinder before. They did, of course. It was the same with the vast areas that belonged to particular Water Boards. Walkers weren't allowed because of the fear of contamination of the water, so no one could walk around Derwent – officially! People used to keep a look-out for the Game-keepers and the Game-keepers were doing the same, trying to catch people.

I thought the access agreements were a good thing. Most people involved in walking and climbing thought they were. On Stanage,for instance, although that was private land, hundreds of people used to use it for climbing. Stanage and Wharncliffe Crags, which are very close to Sheffield, were the very first two rock areas to be used by climbers. Climbing, rock climbing, really started in Sheffield in the mid-twenties when people were out of work and had a lot of time on their hands. Stanage was within walking distance and it was a new sport that started. Even today there are more climbers in Sheffield than anywhere else in the country, even more than Wales and Scotland. Sheffield's always been the centre. People move to Sheffield to be near Stanage. A lot of young people will opt to go to Sheffield University because of Stanage. The Edge is three-and-a-half miles long and you can count about a thousand people there at weekends. That's a lot of people. They queue, literally queue, to get at the climb.

Within the Peak Park it's the most used area because they've got the climbing, paragliding, hang-gliding and, to a certain extent, cross-country motor-cycling. There's a right-of-way by Stanage Pole and you can't stop people taking cars up there.

In the early days Tom Tomlinson was sitting at Stanage Pole in the middle of winter; we seemed to have more severe winters then and there was lots and lots of snow. He was having his lunch and he thought 'That's funny. That's a motor car.' And coming up the old Roman road from Sheffield to Stanage Pole was a bread delivery van. It stopped when it got to Tom and there were two young lads, the driver and the driver's mate, and they said 'Are we all right for Hathersage?'

Tom said 'Yes, you are but why are you here? Burbage is the main road.'

'Oh, well,' they said, 'we couldn't get past Burbage because of the snow, so we came in this way,' and off they went.

Tom always said that, as far as he knew, they'd got to Hathersage.

I walk up there and often there are four-wheel-drive vehicles and cross country motor-cyclists running up and down so it's a very difficult area to look after from the bird point of view.

There were some characters around. At Overstones Farm, when we first started out, the sheep farmer there was Peter Priestley and he was always very keen on ballroom dancing. He was a farmer right out in the moors but he loved ballroom dancing! He never had a car, he had a tractor. And we'd quite often see Peter on his way to a dance, beautifully dressed, driving the tractor.

The foot-and-mouth epidemic in the sixties hit the farmers very, very hard. But in another way it did good, too, because there was always a certain amount of anti between the local people and the farmers and the Park Planning Board. When the foot-and-mouth started we tried not to move the Rangers around too much so we generally kept close to where we were. Most of the time I was asked to stop people going up Redmires and Stanage Edge and in the course of that I got to know Frankie Hammond, who was the local farmer, really well and Frankie became a really good, close friend. And that happened a lot. I think after that, after the foot-and-mouth, there was a lot closer working relationship through-out the park.

Ray Ollerenshaw used to say he had much more respect for the Ranger Service because the lads built an igloo up at Derwent and that stayed right through that winter. That's where the Rangers would shelter because during the foot-and-mouth people would volunteer, if they had a day off work, go out mid-week as well as weekends.

Mr and Mrs Prigent were tenant farmers at North Lees Farm. We were introduced to them and they were very good to us. About nine o'clock in the morning we'd go down to their kitchen, which had a big Aga cooker, and have a cup of tea and a chat. At ten we'd go up on the Edge and come back down to them at maybe half-past-four in the afternoon and dry out in their kitchen. We got to know Mr and Mrs Prigent very well.

Later on, the Peak Park Planning Board built the small briefing centre up above North Lees. We used it for years and years and the Mountain Rescue Team kept their equipment there because we were also founder members of the Edale Mountain Rescue Team.

As Wardens we were getting called out in the middle of the night on rescues and nothing was organised. George Garlick was the full-time Warden in Edale. By then we'd got Field Head, which was a big house where we briefed and George slept, and if anybody was lost or injured over night we were called. I'd set off in the car and my wife would start calling round a few more people and eventually we'd get together. But we realised we'd got to get better organised. We approached the Planning Board and said we wanted to form a Mountain Rescue Team. They were very good and allowed us to use the Board's Land-Rovers and stretchers so we always had a certain amount of equipment at Stanage because there were more rescues, evacuations from Stanage than anywhere else. Most weekends somebody would fall off or sprain an ankle, mostly not serious.

Most of the incidents were funny. Early one morning we were at North Lees Farm talking to Mr and Mrs Prigent and somebody came running down, saying somebody had fallen off The Edge. In those days the stretcher and other bits were at the farm. We gathered the stuff together and got to the top road. We had a Very Pistol which fired 'two star red' which is the standard Mountain Rescue way of alerting people. We didn't need to fire it because the people that were going to be involved were already there but Mr Prigent fired the pistol. It came down into the bracken and set fire to it. It was so funny because we were all dashing around and stamping the fire out before we could get to the person who'd fallen. His friends were saying 'It's about time you arrived. We thought there were Red Indians down there because you were all dancing up and down.'

On one occasion, it was in a really hard winter, David Copley and I had been on Stanage. There was lots of snow about and we got back to the Briefing Centre, made a cup of tea and all the rest of it. We'd got two cars, David and myself in one, I was driving, and another couple of Rangers in another car. We got to the bottom corner and had started going over to Overstones car park when we realised that it was just like glass, solid ice, but we managed to keep going and we got to just beyond Overstones Farm where it eases off a little bit and I stopped. We could still see the headlights of the other car and Dave said he'd get out and see if he could give it a push. 'You just keep the car ticking over.'

In those days we all used to wear very dark, almost black jackets which were ex-Fleet Air Arm jackets, they used to use them on the Aircraft

Carriers during the war. You could buy them for £1.50, thirty shillings in old money. So we were dressed very darkly and it was a dark night and Dave always used to take a pint bottle of milk for our cups of tea. I don't know why but on this occasion he'd still got mugs and milk.

We sat in my car and Dave was holding the bottle of milk and mugs. I got out and both the other lads got out and as soon as Dave's feet touched the floor he started to slide. You can imagine the situation. He's holding a bottle of milk, he's sliding at high speed. It was very misty, foggy, nasty. But they'd got their headlights on and suddenly this apparition came towards them with a bottle of milk that was shining brilliantly white. He just managed to get there and then, of course, he slipped up.

Another time I was sitting by the trig point on Stanage with Frank Eyre, who was a Ranger, and we were looking across the valley. We saw there were two cars being driven over the rough ground, normal cars. I thought, 'That's funny.' Then one of them started accelerating, going faster and faster and faster, and went straight over the cliff and disappeared, just like that.

They were very, very lucky. Coming out of Hathersage at what's called the cupola, they'd come towards this cliff and gone right over. Fortunately, about thirty feet down, there's a little projection and they'd hit it and stopped. They weren't hurt at all. They were two young lads that had just been larking about, hadn't realised ... I don't know what they thought they were doing. Their Guardian Angels were on form!

We used to do quite a lot of patrols on skis. Real chocolate advert stuff! I'll tell you something of winter. The four of us were on duty and we couldn't get the cars up there so we met up at Hunter's Bar in Sheffield and walked out to the Edge. We checked it out to see if there was anybody there and checked for sheep because you could get a lot of them under the Edge and they'd just get covered completely. Like being in an avalanche. We did our normal check and there was nobody else about so we decided we'd walk from Stanage up to Fox House, have our lunch there and then we'd walk back to Sheffield.

At some point Derek, one of the Rangers, fell over and rolled down the hill. He got no sympathy at all. We got to the Toad's Mouth – it's on the

Foxhouse to Hathersage Road and it's a big rock that looks like a toad – then started to go up the main road to the Foxhouse. The snow was as high as this ceiling, probably higher – that's about twelve feet.

Derbyshire County Council had hired a huge snow-plough and eventually we saw it parked outside at Foxhouse. There'd been a VW Passatt parked at the side of the road and the snow-plough had gone right through it. You know how you see these diagramatic drawings of cars? It was just like that, just half a car.

We thought we were the only ones in Foxhouse. We opened the pub door and it was full of water from peoples' boots, but we sat down in the pub, ordered a drink and got our sandwiches out. Derek, the one who'd fallen down, worked in the steel works in Sheffield and somewhere along the line he'd had an accident and lost his hand. He just had a stump. When he'd fallen down he'd badly grazed this stump. We sat down and were eating our sandwiches and we could see people looking. I think they thought he'd just lost his hand!

The same winter Dave and I were walking back from Stanage Edge towards Burbage Bridge, on the main road from Ringinlow. We'd just got to the Bridge and we found we were walking on the roof of a car. A minute or two later Dave's key caught in something and it was the top of a road sign.

The worst one, or the best, whichever way you look at it, was 1947. They had telegraph poles in those days and at Edale the snow was over the top of them, and the Barrel Inn at Hucklow was completely covered for months. It was only the fact they'd a lot of food in that they managed.

Even right down in the east end of Sheffield they were having to put straw down in the streets for the horses to walk on.

A lot of people went up there in their four-wheel-drive Land Rovers. They used to think they could go anywhere. They'd come from Stanadge Pole across the moor which is very, very wet and they used to sink right down to the wheels. Then they'd come to us and say 'Can you help us?'

And we'd say, 'Oh, no. No way.'

We'd phone the Planning Board and they'd send a couple of full-time Rangers out on Monday morning to pull them out and charge them to try to teach them a lesson.

Of course, there were really serious accidents and a few fatalities. The hang-gliding had just started in those days. I suppose they must be a lot more advanced now because they can strap themselves in. Back then, if they lost control they seemed to come down face first. We picked up one or two. It was a mess. And that's the way it went for a long, long time. We always kept busy. By then we'd got the radios so we were able to contact the Police and then they'd contact the ambulance service which would either come from Bakewell or, more usually, from Sheffield.

One time a couple came in with a little girl, she was probably about five or six. They'd just been out walking and she'd been running around a little bit and had just collapsed. It was in winter, at night, and her lips were terribly blue. She'd got heart problems. We kept giving her mouth to mouth for an hour or so before we got the doctor up from Hathersage and then the ambulance and they got her as far as the hospital in Sheffield but she died. Those things you tend to remember.

But a lot of people used to rely on that little building there. They knew, whatever happened, they could dash down there and we could do something, that we'd got the radio and we could get in touch with a doctor down in Hathersage.

They were pioneering days really. The Peak Park was a blue-print for all the parks that came after it. Still is. They've won a lot of awards over the years and I think they're still the leaders in many, many ways.

There's been changes over the years and they're for the good. Half the population of the country live within sixty miles of the park and some weekends it feels as if they've all decided to come! So there've been all sorts of problems out here that you wouldn't necessarily get in some of the other National Parks, purely because of the volume.

Before I joined the Ranger Service, when we had the little cottage, it was really busy. People were working mainly in factories in Sheffield and Manchester and they just wanted to get out for their weekends. When you got back to Edale Station after a days walk, say on a Sunday, both platforms were packed, and I really mean end to end. One side would be the Manchester people, on the other side were the Sheffield people.

What makes it so popular? I think for one thing, certainly for the Sheffield people, it's the availability of the place. And there's any amount of things you can do. Everybody's not interested in climbing, obviously, but there's a lot of family walks. People can take their cars up to Redmires reservoir and they've got the options of several walks.

And there's a lot of history there. The area was used for training round about the Napoleonic wars and people have found cannon balls and lead shot.

Near the upper reservoir, nearest to Stanage, there's a hill called Hill 60. In the First World War there was a hill in Belgium which was fought over for a long, long time and a lot of people were killed, and that was Hill 60. It was 60 metres high and the hill at Redmires is named after it. All round the top is where they simulated the trenches.

There's a Prisoner-of-War camp on Redmires Hill which is roughly where the old Roman Road is. It started at Templeborough, came up and over Stanage Edge, down in to Hathersage and across the Hope Valley which is where there's the remains of another Roman fort, and from there over to Buxton.

After that there were the Salters. Roman soldiers were paid in salt because it was very important. They had to have salt to live. All the salt was produced in Cheshire, still is, I think. In those days they used to produce the salt and then men with pack-horses would bring it from Cheshire right over the Pennines to the Doncaster area where a lot of it was then put on barges and would be exported. The area had severe winters and you can imagine the pack-horses with heavy loads of salt. They still had to be able to find their way over so they had a series of posts and Stanage Pole was the last one. This was round about the late seventeen-hundreds. As far as I know Stanage Pole is the only one left.

The grindstones that are the symbol of the National Park were produced in the Stanage area. That went on in the eighteen-hundreds when they were used particularly in Sheffield for grinding cutlery.

So there's a lot of history up there. That's the thing. The Park's got everything. Landscapes, views, big areas of water and history. I go on holidays all over the place but I come back, I always look forward to

Snow form on Stanage Edge © Peak District National Park Authority

Walkers on Stanage
© Peak District National Park Authority

coming back. Never tire of it. It's incredible.

Bill Darley

Ted Ellerton has walked the moors from the 1940's. When disaster struck he must have wondered if he would ever again stride out over Stanage.

My favourite walk is from Hathersage, through Bretton Clough, up to Bretton and circling round Eyam and back again – with a compulsory stop at the old pub, The Barrel! It's changed a lot since the old days but it's a fantastic pub. Years ago my wife and I were members of the Youth Hostel Association and we always came back to Lodge Moor across Stanage.

In the 1940's I was a bus driver and on my two rest days I could guarantee I went out walking. I belonged to a club that is extinct now, the Sheffield Rambling Club that was a breakaway group from the Clarion. I've belonged to other rambling clubs too, even one down at Derby, the Allestree Ramblers. I was married down there. She died – passed away ...

We both loved Stanage. It seems still as it was years ago before they started making the grinding stones around that area. It's still the same. It's just the grandeur of the area. Looking round there in all weathers, be it snowy or raining or the sun's shining, it's just great. The only trouble is that if there's a wind you've got to get on your hands and knees or else you'd get blown off. I walked on the top, still do, and I've been down on my hands and knees many a time. It's exhilarating, though, as long as you've got your waterproofs on and good warm clothing

And it's so interesting because there's stones where the old Landowners had them hollowed out for watering the birds. A fair number there is up there. The rain drops into the stones and they hold the water for the grouse. Each one's numbered. They're still there now. When the weather was dry people used to fill them with water and the estate owners paid them a half-penny for each one. They are part of the history of Stanage.

I've slept wild up there many a time. Without a tent sometimes.

I used to cook directly on a stone. In the old days ramblers used to carry a frying pan on their haversack and they'd carry some sausage or liver and onions and stuff and cook it directly on a stone.

I don't get out quite as much now, not since I lost my sight, but I'm going tomorrow with the Chesterfield Ramblers. It'll be a short one, five miles, five-and-a-half, something like that. A short one, that. I did seven miles last Wednesday. I've done ten and twelve miles as a blind person.

I lost my first eye in 1994 and then the other one in February 1997. Woke up blind. Yes, woke up blind. The car was parked outside, the haversack was ready for walking and my pack-up was in the fridge.

I had to get someone to take me to the Hallamshire and I ended up at Queen's Medical Centre in Nottingham. The operation gave me partial sight but it deteriorated within nine months. There's nothing there now.

Emma, my guide dog, doesn't always come with me because she's only young, just over two years old, so I can't put her on long walks where it's rough. She's used to walking on pavements but she was trained especially for me to walk in the countryside. Trained with sheep and cows.

I'll take her next Thursday when we go to Ladybower and she'll walk under control and she'll ignore the sheep. She'll walk within six or seven inches of one, just walk past it, won't even bark all day. It's a rest day for her. She's got a lovely nature, she's a good companion and she's the best exercised guide dog in the country!

I started 'Walking for the Visually Impaired' in Sheffield.

When I went blind I was absolutely frustrated at not getting out. I didn't have Emma then and I'd been taught to walk with a tactile cane, the long white cane that folds up. I just couldn't get anywhere and it meant walking at a slow speed as well.

Being used to being outdoors and losing my sight was a bit like an ordinary chap or a lady losing their legs. I had a talk with the Visual Impairment team in Sheffield and my Welfare Officer who took me down to a meeting of the Ramblers Association in Sheffield. I gave a talk to them about the difficulties I was facing. They considered it and in the April of 2000 we took our first walk and we've been walking ever since with the assistance of the Ramblers Association guides. Some guides don't belong to the RA, even a lady from Nottingham comes along and guides us sometimes.

Similar schemes were already running in other places. Derby and Chesterfield had already got them running and they had a marvellous one down in London. But they only walk in summer-time. They join in with a rambling club and the men and women from the club act as guides.

I'm quite pleased to have set it up because we've met people who've never been walking in the countryside before – they've sat in their flats or houses, whatever – elderly people, some in their fifties and sixties, and they've finally got out. They've been encouraged to get out. It's been advertised through the Radio – I've been on the radio.

We get them to buy some cheap rambling boots that are waterproof and they love it. They're really grateful for being out there, they really are, just to feel the wind on their faces and hear the sound of the birds and the chatter. They're a happy lot, they're always laughing. It's fantastic. I'm really happy about it.

Another RA member, an American lady who's partially sighted, is a prominent worker in Visually Impaired circles. Without her it wouldn't be happening. I started it but she keeps it going. She's not a really strong walker, she won't do a twelve mile walk, but she'll do seven or eight. She does it at her own speed and she thoroughly enjoys being out.

The guides take it in turns and change over at break time when we have our pack-up. That's if we've got enough guides. We can always do with more.

I can remember being on Stanage with one guide for two visually impaired people. In bad weather! It was really exhilarating, as it happens. We met other people that knew us and they wondered how we'd got there. We enjoyed it. It was fantastic. We haven't had an accident yet, touch wood.

I feel safe with someone guiding me. I get to stride out a bit, to walk quicker than I would be able to if I was walking on my own anywhere. The ground surface is always uncertain, especially at places like Stanage, but if you have decent boots on – that's the thing – if people are adequately shod and clothed, they're ok.

I'm always catching myself, always knocking my hands. You can't help it. You walk along and you can't see and you catch a post. The guide is on the right-hand side of me, walking, and he or she doesn't realise there's a stone coming three foot from the ground. Just one of those things.

My guide describes it to me. He'll ask me if I remember so-and-so, or a certain stone or whatever, and I'll tell him 'yes', maybe a way-mark, the old way-marks from the old days when they used to bring the salt over from Cheshire with their ponies. There's some stones at Longshaw. Some have been moved because of making proper roads but some are still in their original positions to mark the lay-out of the lanes.

And at the same time we're getting all the smells and sounds around us, the birds. It's fantastic. Got to use your imagination sometimes.

I used to be an amateur photographer, I did slide shows and things like that. So I used to stop many a time on a ramble and I'd be taking pictures. And even now the official rambling clubs like to get from A to B in as quick a time as possible but they miss quite a lot. They get the exhilaration of getting there fast but ...

There's a lot to see. All kinds of things, even different kinds of grasses. Until I lost my sight I didn't know they were there but you can feel and touch things. So tactile. Great.

I don't know what I'd do if I couldn't go. It's fantastic. The outdoors is fantastic and Stanage area is really something spectacular. It's on its own, isn't it?

I wrote this song with Sally Goldsmith for the Year of the Artist.

Just after the war I moved here to Sheffield
While I was still a young man
I'd not been here long when I started to ramble
And I still do whenever I can.

I took my first walk with a pal at a weekend
Me with me Army boots on
An old jacket, a pair of suit trousers
Up to Stocksbridge, the Dan and the Don.

I worked six days a week on the old Sheffield buses
And the week it was hard and so long
Then I met with a chap who had been in the Army
And he loved a good walk and a song.

It was through this mate Roy that I joined Sheffield Ramblers
And in this club they loved a good sing
We'd end up in a pub with a few beers inside us
And our chorus would make the hills ring.

The Barrel at Bretton, the Greyhound at Warslow
The Foxhouse and pubs in the dale
The locals all knew us, our fame spread before us
In the Inns on the moors and the dales.

The closeness of friends and the swell of our voices
In harmony we'd sing along
Oh the first pratty flowers and our own Sheffield Ramblers
Each man had his favourite song.

Oh now I've no sight I still sing and I ramble
I wander from here and to there
I smell the wet leaves and I hear the sweet birdsong
Feel the rain on my face and my hair.

So don't write us off or exclude the old ramblers
If we're slow on our legs or can't see
We still want to hike and we'll stand up and say so
So support us to walk and roam free.

Just after the war I moved here to Sheffield
While I was just a young man
I'd not been here long when I started to ramble
And I still do whenever I can.

Ted Ellerton

In 1915 Charles Chandler wrote: 'There is a freedom at Stanadge that you do not get in the same degree anywhere else on the moors ... Nothing seems to stand between you and absolute joy in the invigorating air and the unique views of moor, mountain, and peaceful valley. The city is behind you, and the world is your own.'

He sums up the feelings of the members of the Sheffield Ramblers Association who regularly walk Stanage. Many of them belong to other walking groups, including Left Foot Forward and an all women's group. Because walking is such an integral part of their lives, some of them are guides for partially sighted and blind people, enabling them to continue to have the freedom of walking the moors.

Stanage still has a wildness, a solitude, despite the numbers of people that use it. When I first started climbing Stanage regularly, in the early 1950's, I could count the people I saw on one hand, even on a Sunday. Now there are hundreds of people there but still, in the week, you can walk from Lodge Moor and, if you follow a certain route, you can walk for two or three hours right along Stanage and not meet anybody.

It's wonderful up there in the snow because there are no footprints, you're the first person to walk on it and you can come back two hours later and there's still only your own footprints.

To me Stanage is unique in that it's within a few feet of the Sheffield City boundary, almost in Sheffield City. You wouldn't think that a large city like Sheffield would have such beautiful countryside within its boundary. Yet there's one place, under High Neb, just twenty yards from the Edge, and you can sit there and see nothing but the landscape; no buildings, no barns, no roads.

Some of the Sheffield Ramblers walk with people with visual impairment, enabling them to taste the freedom of Stanage.

I've led walks for people with visual impairment right across Stanage. They are part of the Ramblers Association and some of them are better walkers than I am; stronger, fitter. They love going on the moors because although they've lost their sight they sense so much from the surrounding area. They can tell when they're on the moors. They can tell when they're going through a wood. They can hear the streams. Some of them bring their guide dogs with them for a day out in the countryside when they don't have to work.

Not everybody wants to be a guide so it is done on a purely voluntary basis. We have two of these walks a month and each person needs a helper. We get a lot out of it and so do the walkers, so everyone enjoys the walk.

Many people see Stanage as a special place but for one organisation it has a particularly strong bond.

I went on Stanage for my first walk in 1943 and I've been going back ever since because we have the Rock of Resolution in Stanage. That's where the Sheffield Woodcraft Folk were first formed on April 10th 1929, during a trespass ramble to Stanage Edge. The Rock of Resolution is where twelve members of the Independent Labour Party, as it was then, met and said they wanted to start an organisation for children. They'd heard of one in London, in fact it had been running since 1925, and they felt it was the type of organisation they wanted to form to get the children out of the city. At that time the city was smoke; you could stand on Stanage Edge and see an absolute smoke barrier right across the city. The organisation was based on the work of Ernest Thompson-Seton who had lived amongst the Sioux Indians of America. He worked with deprived children in the late 1880's and the Sheffield Woodcraft Folk intended to work with children who were living in poverty following the First World War.

We have to use different names whenever we are with the Folk to promote the equality that is one of the founding principles of the organisation. At the first camp fire you write your given name on a piece of Birch bark and burn it in the fire. You never use it again. I was known as Brown Bear, then there was Badger and Beaver.

Groups sprang up all over Sheffield and worked with children, both boys and girls, from six years old. The six to ten year olds were the Elfins, the 11-15 year olds were Pioneers and the over sixteens were Kinsfolk.

They were encouraged to take on any jobs that needed doing and to enjoy craft work, singing, dancing and games.

We even held marriage and christening ceremonies there. The people would have had the ceremonies made legal at the Register Office or Church but the actual ceremony, held outside, was a Woodcraft Folk one.

My wife and I used to take our daughter with us, in her pram. We pushed her from Lodge Moor, over Stanage and down the Edge. We even took a portable gramophone up there for Folk Dancing.

During the war Sheffield Folk members worked with Folk from London to form a refugee escape route out of Czechoslovakia for children. Our President at the time, who had formed the Woodcraft Folk, brought one of the young girls over here to live with him. He still lives in Sheffield and she goes on the anniversary outings with him.

The Woodcraft Folk have high principles and are willing to stand by them, even at risk to themselves. They took action again Fascism in Britain, attending a rally at the Sheffield City Hall where Oswald Mosley was giving a speech to the Blackshirts. Several of the Sheffield Folk who had pacifist sympathies were imprisoned for refusing to fight in the Second World War.

Over the years the organisation has changed to reflect the world and society as it is but the Woodcraft Folk don't have as much involvement now. At one time we brought children out from the Sheffield estates but people don't really want to work with difficult children and teenagers. I'm still involved though and we still celebrate our anniversaries.

'I may be a wage slave on Monday but I am a free man on Sunday..' Ewen Maccoll – Folk Singer who wrote of the Mass Trespasses.

The Campaign for Access made a strong impression and, to this day, is written about in the press. As the Guardian newspaper reported, the mass trespass was a victory of the ordinary folk over the establishment.

The police and gamekeepers knew we were going to trespass and were there waiting for us but they never did anything. If they had it would just have given us more publicity.

Initially it was just walkers and ramblers who felt so strongly about the issue but the harsh treatment that was handed out, including prison sentences, led to the general public supporting us.

What it came down to was the land-owners wanted to keep their land for field sports; fishing, shooting, hunting. They were never going to willingly give us access.

But things have changed. Not all land-owners are against us now. In fact The Duke of Devonshire is opening another sixty-five miles of moor. He's one of the few so called enlightened landowners.

At an anniversary meeting for the Campaign for Access he was on the platform with a man who was put in prison in 1934 for going onto land. The Duke of Devonshire said 'I want to apologise to these people for what my ancestors did to them in the 1930's. I want to apologise for everything they did because I know now that it was wrong.'

That's a terrific step forward.

The Sheffield Ramblers

Sheffield in war time; factories and railways were targeted, buildings bombed, people made homeless.

What could be more natural than a longing to get out of the city and into the countryside? That is exactly what Madge and Ron Townsend did. Madge was working at Samuel Osborn and Company when she began walking with a group of friends.

We began Youth Hostelling, then we fancied climbing and a lady who worked in the Post Room at Osborns put us in touch with Jack McLeod who was a member of the old Sheffield Climbing Club. We met most Sundays and loved it. He introduced us to other members of his club; Rupert Brookes, who has a climb named after him on Burbage, Eric Byne and Freda Rylatt. She was the Chief Librarian at Duke Street Library in Sheffield.

Our mates thought that we were a bit 'way out', which is what we wanted to be! Eventually we bought our own rope and decided we would try to be independent of the men. Peggy Coates and myself actually did some leading and on longer climbs we would lead-through. There weren't many climbers at that time and everyone knew everyone else. We met up with a group of young climbers who seemed to be doing great things and before long we all became acquainted. It was a great surprise when we discovered that several of the group also worked at Osborn's at the bottom of the Wicker in the Lower Yard Melting Plant.

The meeting of the girls and young men on Stanage was to have far-reaching effects; for Madge and Ron it was the beginning of a partnership that has endured. Not that it was a foregone conclusion. Madge went out with several of the young men before she and Ron became a couple.

Ron was in the Home Guard and had to be on duty on Sunday mornings so I tried to organise with my friends to always be on Stanage, as it was the most accessible crag, so that he could join us on Sunday afternoon. He'd either cycle over or come on the Lodge Moor bus.

Ron takes up the story that led to the forming of a new club and publication of a guide.

In 1942 myself and a small group of climbing friends decided to form a climbing club in Sheffield. The first official meeting took place during the last weekend that the Derwent Youth Hostel was open. It was decided it should be called the Peak Climbing Club and it's still going strong now with a membership of fifty-plus who are very active and organise several social events as well as the climbing meets. We originally had members from the Manchester area but now they come mainly from the Sheffield and district area. When Madge and her friends began climbing with us on a regular basis we opened the club to women for the first time.

There were enough climbs to keep us going, a wide variation. It's the finest gritstone edge. Really fantastic.

Madge and I still go to the annual dinner and the 50th Anniversary of the club was celebrated with several overseas members joining us. We celebrated our 60th Anniversary last year.

In the 40's there weren't many climbing guide books in print. I was a

Ron Townsend leading on Rusty Wall
© Hubert Courtney-Bryson

Madge Townsend (nee Cobb) belaying Peggy
Siddons (nee Coates) on Jigger Face
© Ron Townsend

member of the first Gritstone Guide Committee which was formed in 1946 and held at the Engineers Club in Manchester. It was chaired by Eric Byne and included Harry Harley, Birtwistle and Norman Horsfield, all famous names in climbing circles. Once the committee was formed we met at the County Council Offices in Matlock.

Climbing was an important area of our lives. I've even got a climb named after me; Townsend's Variation.

My work in climbing led on to other things. In the early 1950's I received a letter from Jack Longland, then the Director of Education for Derbyshire, saying that my name had been put forward by Alf Bridges regarding the setting up of an Open Air Pursuits Centre at Buxton. It was to be called Whitehall and is going now.

I was a voluntary instructor there from 1950 to 1970 and that was where I met other young instructors who have since become famous climbers like Doug Scott and the Burgess twins.

Things have changed over the years; proper climbing boots rather than plimsoles, strong rope instead of hemp and the amount of gear a climber has round their waist is amazing.

The numbers of climbers has increased, a lot of people doing very hard routes. Very technical gear being used – things we never even thought of, a lot of good protection which enables much harder routes to be climbed safely.

Gritstone is very hard and as we got older we found it more so. The amount of courage some of the young climbers display today is bewildering; it's almost a gymnastic sport.

We haven't really been part of the climbing scene during the last few years but we've not given up entirely. I actually led a climb in the Lake District when I was 79. I'd done it for the first time in 1943 and enjoyed it very much. I'd always dreamed about repeating it. Dave Gregory, a climbing friend of mine, accompanied me up to the lakes and we did South-west on Pillar – very severe grade.

After a lifetime of climbing and walking Stanage is still very special to us. We spent hours there and they were wonderful days.

Madge and Ron Townsend

Ron Townsend on Jigger Face 2002
© David Wright

TALKING HEADS

Gordon Stainforth, author, photographer, film maker and climber, and *Freda Raphael, historical researcher and climber* in conversation.

Stanage is one of my favourite places. It's in a lovely setting, particularly around High Neb, and technically the hardest climbs are comparable to the hardest climbs in the world, yet it's got something for everybody; it's every grade that is high quality, so it's very good for beginners too. A lot of people would argue it's the best crag overall in the Peak District. The whole of the history of English rock-climbing is represented there, too. All the big names.

I started rock climbing when I was at the University of East Anglia which is just about as far from the crag as you can get! We used to pile into the Student Union van on a Friday night and come up to the Peak District as often as possible.

    Stanage really was outstanding. About that time there weren't many women climbing and I was very, very keen. One Boxing Day, it must have been 1968 or '69, the bloke I went around with at the time and a lecturer from the University went up on toStanage Edge with me. We were the only people on the crag because it was not only Boxing Day but there was a horizontal blizzard. We couldn't get very much done because the lecturer got stuck and we had to spend the rest of the day rescuing him from a ledge that was rapidly filling up with snow. Another weekend there's me and eleven blokes. I went to lead up this little climb. Up until then I'd only ever climbed severe or hard severe, and a chap came over saying 'What the f... are you doing here?' At that time you wouldn't have said things like that, you just didn't talk to people like that, and I went into a complete wobble. I was all of a shake. All these chaps I was climbing with drew up round me and all stood shoulder to shoulder and said 'She's with us.'

It's very interesting the way things have changed and that is one of the big differences. Now there are so many women climbing. It isn't just that socially things have changed, as they have, it's that it has got much, much safer. In the sixties, up until about 1967/68, it was still pretty dangerous climbing at Stanage because you couldn't protect a lot of the climbs at all well and if you fell off you hit the ground. It's quite rocky; there were quite a few fatalities in the early days in proportion to the number of people climbing. Now there's all the modern protection. It all came of age about the mid-seventies. The gear was suddenly so much better and things that used to be terrifying were suddenly ok – Black Slab, (Hargreave's route) which we used to walk past hoping no one was going to mention it, was given the lowly grade of severe and it had no protection on it at all. A lot of people had hurt themselves on that and I think a few people had died on it. In the sixties a thing like that was terrifying. Now it's completely safe. You get about four very good runners in and it's gone up to VS and it's much easier to climb. The whole place is much friendlier.

I started climbing in big boots, not flat-soled rock boots, and a thin hemp waist-line which was twenty feet. You wrapped it round and round your waist and tied the last bit in a reef-knot. Then you put a big krab through the whole thickness of the rope. Hemp tends to rot from the inside out and this is why you had such a length wrapped round you, so that if it snapped you were unlikely to unravel.

I fell off on a hemp waist-line. It was just at the end of the time when there was no alternative. The rope jammed and I was under an overhang. It was extremely painful Because you're on a waist line you don't sit, you hang, you hang in the middle of your body.

There's also the thing about the diaphram, you've got about twenty minutes...

Emlyn Jones was running along underneath me and he kept saying 'Try and get the rope free, Freda. You've got fifteen minutes to live.'

I was desperately trying to heave myself upright on this rope and trying to free it on the overhang where it was jammed.

I can't remember how I got out but I did eventually. It was horrendous, so painful.

The point about it was that it was fine – it would hold you. But if you ended up below an overhang without a waist-line you hadn't got long to live if you got stuck. So a big breakthrough was sit-harnesses where there are loops round your thighs as well. The modern climbing harness bears no resemblance to them, it's just so much better.

And the whole way you now belay people is completely different. In the old days you used to just wear gardening gloves, you had the rope round your waist and it was quite easy to drop people. I dropped someone once on Curbar Edge and they landed rather heavily. Now we've got these incredible modern belay devices that don't require any strength at all. The rope just locks. The main thing is the running belays, all these little wire nuts, called rocks. Where in the old days you couldn't put on anything now you can get something that would just about hold a double-decker bus, it's so strong.

Then there were two other breakthroughs – one was what you are actually climbing with on your feet – that's got progressively better – and there was a huge leap forward, again late seventies, with this modern sticky rubber. It isn't rubber at all, it's exactly what they use on aircraft tyres. A guy in Spain had this brilliant idea of using what aircraft fighters have on their wheels. He decided to try an assignment of that stuff and rock-climbing changed almost overnight. Everyone went up one full grade with those new sticky boots.

The equipment is a major thing and it's why a place like Stanage is so popular. Limestone has always remained more serious. It's much, much safer than it used to be but...

The Peak is limestone and gritstone and they are utterly different, about as different as two rocks could be in close proximity. Totally different climbing syles. Limestone will never become a big, popular family type of thing whereas at Stanage you get families out there with their dogs, toddlers doing their first climb, everyone is there and there's a fantastic atmosphere.

It never used to be like that, it used to be much grimmer, more a place for experts, particularly in the thirties and late forties. With all this modern gear everyone is now having a go at much harder stuff.

There's some very interesting historical points, too. One important aspect is the big access problem that existed before the Peak District became a National Park in 1951. People were not allowed to walk and climb in the area. On Stanage the keepers were quite friendly but in other areas you weren't allowed to go there at all and it has been known for keepers to beat up people who were 'trespassing'. Basically, if you saw the keepers coming you just skedaddled and no one would do anything. Some people asked for permission, pulled strings.

Around the First World War there was a little bunch of about twenty of them, including the American Consulate in Sheffield, Rice Kemper Evans, who invented the word 'layback' which is a very general climbing term. They were just a bunch of nutters. A lot of them were killed in the First World War. It was very quiet in the early twenties but some amazing things were done. A thing like Kelly's Overhang, which is now given E1, they tried that for about a decade. Kelly himself didn't do it. Even then standards were being pushed so that something like Kelly's Overhang in 1926 would have been as hard as any rock climb in the world at that date, technically.

A lot of people wandering around now in the park assume it has always been this nice leisure place. It has not. The world before and after the Second World War was utterly different. It was like a different planet. As I say, very few people – they were regarded as 'the masses' – were risking it because they weren't allowed on there. It tended to be the upper-class with connections but in the thirties you did get a few working class people. But there was never actually a class thing in climbing. In the old clubs, like the Rucksack club in Manchester, it didn't matter where you came from, so even in those days it cut right across class. Of course, a lot of the working class people were tougher and stronger because they had manual, labouring jobs and I think by even the thirties there were quite a few working class climbers. After the Second World War came complete revolution.

The Labour government came in and the National Park was born and that's when people like Joe Brown appeared on the scene.

Immediately all the Oxbridge types were kicked into touch in terms of ability. It was the Mancunians in those days who stole the show and the whole standard of rock-climbing went up by one giant leap from 1948 onwards.

Joe Brown and his mates led the way, people like Don Whillans. There was a whole bunch of them and Joe Brown was a superstar. The beginning of his achievement at Stanage is represented by one climb, the Right Unconquerable. They'd been trying in the thirties many, many times and no one could do it, and Joe Brown – I think he was seventeen – goes up to the bottom and does it. He does the Left Unconquerable first, which had been rumoured to have been done before although my research now suggests it hadn't been, followed by the Right Unconquerable, on sight, and that was so gobsmacking that every one was talking about it. Then he went on National Service so this amazing new superstar disappeared for about a year. When he came back he completely changed the course of British rock-climbing – but mostly in Snowdonia and in the big mountains. He climbed the third highest mountain in the world, Katchenjunga.

It shows that someone whose climbing had started right here in the Peak District, and mostly at Stanage Edge, then went on to become a world name.

I got Joe Brown to repeat Right Unconquerable in 1997 at the age of 67 and that was very exciting for me because he doesn't actually like publicity very much. Amazingly he really has never been someone who's blown his own trumpet and tried to publicise his stuff, and his achievement is probably greater than anybody's in the whole history of rock-climbing for the number of sheer classic routes he's done. Look through any guide book on North Wales and the Peak District right through the fifties and sixties! Anyhow, he doesn't like publicity very much, he still just likes climbing. I managed to get him after a year of talking to him on and off, and he came to repeat Right Unconquerable. That was absolutely fabulous. We were sitting in the café 'Outside', at Hathersage, and I had a couple of friends helping me. I said quietly, 'If people in this café knew what was going to be happening in about an hour's time they'd be amazed. There'd be such a crowd up there.'

To get the photograph I was hanging from a rope just to the right of where he would be, where I could move up and down, so that I could get him at the best angle. We were all in position and there was no sign of Joe at the appointed time. I was getting very worried because he was due to be there at eleven and it was about quarter-past eleven, twenty-past eleven and I'm thinking 'Oh God, what's gone wrong?' Then I saw this little figure with grey hair, and his mate, coming very fast up the Plantation and I just knew straight away that was him. Even from that distance you could see he was someone quite old, just by the way he was moving. He arrived at the bottom, hardly said a thing; very quiet, very professional.

He said 'Hallo Gordon. I might not be able to do this.' He'd hurt his shoulder. He starts off and he launches off up the rock, just as he'd done in the famous picture in 1949, and as soon as he'd done that this sort of grin appeared on his face and as he's going up it he's looking happier and happier. When he gets to the top, he belays and he's just chatting to me. Suddenly he's telling me all these stories and his mate, Claude Davies, is struggling and Joe's taking no notice of Claude at all. He's just telling me these stories. He's just sitting at the top. His mate's dangling, the rope's absolutely tight, then the rope would go slack and he's still talking to me and almost like punctuation, whilst he's talking he's taking in the rope and you'd hear these distant cries.

'What do you do here, Joe?'

He's an amazing character. He has a sort of charisma and a presence that is very hard to explain. He is someone very special indeed and a complete enthusiast.

He's a champion of the sport and there's no-one that's been climbing in the extreme severe grade longer than he has, and he's still doing it. Certainly he was climbing Extreme four years ago so that has to be, by definition, the longest time span of someone climbing at that standard from 1948 up to at least 2000.

There aren't many other sports where you can be good at your sport well into your sixties and even into your seventies. This is something you notice going round this crag. There are a lot of elderly people who are still climbing. It keeps you fit, it keeps you supple and it keeps you mentally alert. There are very few sports that I can think of where that applies. If you're a footballer, for instance... when you're thirty you're past it.

Climbing is special because, okay – a lot of the sports do involve adrenalin but climbing does in particular. It's a natural drug that the body produces and it's a fact that if you have produced a lot of adrenalin during the day you feel fantastic. It's this weird mixture of things. It's why you never get tired of climbing. I'm someone who's quite a nervous climber, I get quite scared, but then, as it starts to go well, you get this incredible high. They call it something like the 'Runners High' or the 'Athletes High' and it is very good for you. It's very good for your head, psychologically, because there's no room in your mind for anything else while you're climbing. You've got to concentrate on that. And actually, contrary to what you might think, it's incredibly relaxing.

No matter how many worries you have, they all go out of the window. You've got to concentrate on what you're doing or you come off.

Climbing at its best has a sort of dream-like quality, too. It's not quite like normal life. When you are doing something near your limit you really are concentrating and you go through into a slightly different dimension. Particularly if it is right at your limit and if it gets dangerous, where if you fall off you are going to hurt yourself. Typically, if it gets dangerous you do pull it out of the bag and you become larger than yourself as a person. You do something you didn't think you were capable of. It's extraordinary.

It's not competitive, you don't defeat anybody. You only win against yourself.

My favourite climb? That's a terribly difficult question. It has to be a list of climbs because there is such variety and such a range of standards. Everything from the smooth slabs, all about balance and friction, to very gymnastic, muscular overhanging stuff. Then there's cracks of every description; very, very thin, to cracks you can get your whole body into, desperately strenuous things, a lot of hand-jamming. Every crack under the sun is represented there. It's very hard to say what is the best. I mean, Right Unconquerable – we have a star system for guide books; three stars means absolutely exceptional, fantastic, totally fascinating; one star means very good and two means extremely good. They tend to be a bit liberal with the stars and unfortunately everyone goes for the starred routes. Right Unconquerable is given three stars but I think, on that system, it should be given four stars. And there are a few like Cave Innominate with Harding's Superdirect which are very good routes.

Years ago we used to finish off the weekend doing the Fairy Steps.
   You could get one tiny little wire in near the beginning. Did you do the Fairy Steps?

Do you know, I didn't have the guts! No protection.

You get up to a certain height then there's a traverse off to the left and you have to step up very delicately. You could easily come off at that point. If you did, you went into this huge pendulum swing and you just didn't hit the ground!

There's some very good routes around Robin Hood's Cave, which, of course, has an extraordinary history of its own. I've done a lot of research into Robin Hood and I believe there *was* a real Robin Hood. Okay – a lot of other myths got latched on to this real Robin, but there were certainly robbers and outlaws living up there in those caves. Stanage is the border between Derbyshire and Yorkshire and it's even more subtle than that, in that the bit of Yorkshire is a place called Hallamshire. It was a very clever place to hang out as an outlaw, you just hopped over the border. And by literally coming out of the top of the chimney at the top of Robin Hood's cave you were in Yorkshire. Come out at the bottom and you were in Derbyshire.
   I think most of the best climbs are within about 200 yards of Robin Hood's Cave. Inverted V, a VS total classic, Hargreave's Original Route, (Black Slab,) that used to be one of these very dangerous things that people used to die on. April Crack – Christmas Crack, now that's classic because people go up on Christmas Day to climb it whatever the weather. It's one of those nonsensical things.
   The other sports have taken off too and the para-gliding and hang-

gliding is, I think, in total harmony with the environment. You don't see it that often, obviously the conditions have to be just right, and it's all happening at the same time, no-one is interfering with anyone else. You can be on a climb and you hear this faint buzzing noise. It's the sound they make as they're soaring backwards and forwards along the Edge and it's lovely because it's just using the wind and the landscape to make it work. I'm really in favour of that. It's wonderful.

Sadly, all the activity damages the rock. It's really hard rock, millstone grit, almost like granite, but however careful people are it gets damaged. Even though we're wearing modern shoes rather than nailed boots it wears the rock and the reason it wears it is that it's not proper rubber, it's got carborundum in it.

The rock stands up to it remarkably well. Limestone gets polished in a matter of a few years. Climbers wreck it. No-one realises that. The climbers realise that by climbing limestone they are wrecking it for themselves, not for anyone else. It looks just the same. Stanage looks the same but everything gets more rounded and in some places it gets a camming device putting tremendous force on flakes. A flake is a type of crack where it's a chunk of rock going obliquely. If you've got a cam behind a flake and a heavy person falls off, it could snap.

If you climb on a crag regularly you disturb any bird life.

If Stanage Edge was just left and nobody was allowed to approach it, it would be colonised by ravens and you'd get vegetation growing in the cracks again.

Things like Holly Tree Crack and Holly Wall got their names because there used to be a holly tree there and I can remember it. We used to belay on the holly tree and put our backs against it to help us get up. But they've long since gone.

Years ago people would strip all the ivy off a crag and go up with a trowel and wire brush and dig all the plants out of the grooves, especially on limestone.

But that damage only happens were there's heavy use. There's a lot of crags where very few people climb and if they've come into vogue with the climbers and some of the vegetation's gone, then they go out of fashion, does nature take over? Yes. It comes bouncing right back.

Stanage is in good hands because there's a very responsible attitude from climbers and the BMC. There's even a whole committee just for Stanage, and climbers, unlike any other activity or walk of life that I know, are by and large fantastically responsible.

There's very little litter on Stanage and most stuff has been left by accident. A lot of people just want to preserve it for the wonderful place it is without it having to get more regulated. It's very good as it is, the balance is just right. No big signs telling you not to do this, not to do that. It's already under control.

And it represents rock-climbing at it's purest. You climb the crag, you use these little wire nuts, whatever. The second tape runners takes them out. There's nothing left. And for a crag that size, yes – there's a few bits and bobs that get stuck and jammed in cracks – but generally it is left in just the state it was found in. And you are not, absolutely not, allowed to put any pegs in now. That tradition's always been with us. In the thirties and forties, well, in the sixties, they were banging pegs in quite a few things. You can't put bolts in Stanage, although a few have been put there in the past – bolts where you actually drill with a power drill to put the bolt in, which makes the climb absolutely safe. If you fall off there's no danger at all. But it's basically wrecked the rock, turned it into a climbing wall. So Stanage has a very purist tradition, and really, the damage climbing does to the rock is really just a problem for climbers.

Stanage is a constant but is always changing. It is the Mecca for climbers the world over.

To paraphrase Dr Johnson, 'A climber who has got tired of Stanage has got tired of life.'

Gordon Stainforth and Freda Raphael

Mark Goodwin has been learning to climb for the last twenty years and learning to write poetry for the last nineteen. During that time he has made many visits to Stanage Edge and has often contemplated and written about the activity and art of climbing and the places in which it takes place.

His favourite mountain-scapes are British, and Stanage Edge and the gritstone edges of the Peak District are particularly important to him. Mark says that, for him, the shapes of Stanage are a solid record of friendships and that he is most grateful to those people who have shared their knowledge of gritstone.

MUSEUM OF THE STANAGE-OPHONE
by
Mark Goodwin

the climber is dialling the stone

his fingers electrical contacts
the operator is very old   is very patient   the operator is Time
the climber is trying to get through
but the stone holds for the moment are engaged

> *sorry, you have dialled incorrectly, please try again*

dialling dialling dialling   fingerprints ripping

> *can you hold please*

see how he is an ear
the whole ear of himself pressed
against this ancient receiver   the curly flex
of Stanage Edge's length ready

to transmit his question

among receding wires of desire   the climber is dialling

dialling dialling dialling dialling

hear how his skin sees
something beneath
rock's surface

feel how grit rasps   then suddenly

stone-hello stone-hello stone-hello welcome

you are through

to the Stanage-ophone
to Grittish Tellestone
to the Tell-Stone of Motion

through to

rock's survival hotline

the conversation begins

Mark Goodwin

What is it that makes people want to climb a rock face, scramble over boulders or jump off the top of crags with a hang-glider on their backs? Is it simply because it's there or are they pitting themselves against nature in a way that was all too familiar to our forebears but is, by and large, missing from life in the twenty-first century? Or is it the need for an adrenalin rush that goes hand-in-hand with risk-taking? The answer may be a mixture of all of those elements but what is certain is that wherever people take part in sports that have a high risk quota there is the need for other people to rescue them.

Thea Williams on Cave Arete, Stanage
© Nick Smith 2002

Stanage Pole
© Robert Helliwell

The Edale Mountain Rescue Team was formed in 1977. It didn't have a vehicle or a base and team members operated from the backs of their own cars. A few ropes, a stretcher and their own personal equipment was all they had in the way of rescue kits. Now the team has vehicles plus a trailer, a reasonable base and thousands of pounds worth of equipment and they are able to buy team members personal kit.

The Team has a corporate image, professional standards that they operate to and a regime of training that has never been set up before.

In the seventies there were probably less than a dozen call-outs a year and it was a question of 'Are you free?' Now the call-out rate is around eighty to a hundred a year, the team are highly trained and pagers are used to contact the forty people who are available at any one time. All of them, and support workers, are on call twenty-four hours a day, seven days a week and most of them have full-time jobs; mountain rescue is something that happens in their spare time.

The sheer numbers of people who visit Stanage inevitably put a strain on the Mountain Rescue Team. Stanage is a mecca, very popular and always will be, primarily because of the gritstone. It's always been very good; it's clean, it's not brittle or friable, and it's in very good condition. There's comparable climbing places like the Roaches and, when it comes to limestone, Stoney Middleton and Water-cum-Jolly are good but not like Stanage. There's hundreds of different climbs across all the different grades so people can go there anytime and climb and be satisfied. An experienced climber could go on to Stanage and be absolutely fulfilled because there are climbs that would test and stretch him. Equally a beginner could have a fantastic day never having climbed before. The Peak District National Park has increased in popularity and people are much more prepared to push themselves now than they were previously. Twenty-five years ago a climber could be guaranteed to have a climb to himself. Now he wouldn't get an edge to himself mid-week never mind weekends.

Another reason for the increase in the popularity of Stanage is that climbing's been made accessible through the climbing walls that have been built in cities. Sheffield's got two major walls and several local walls and there may well be an increase in call-outs because of the transferring of skills from the indoor walls to the outdoors, which are two very different environments. Technically it isn't any easier to climb an indoor wall rather than a Stanage route but the indoor climbs are in a controlled environment. There is a risk, as there is with outdoor climbing, but there may be ropes attached to the top that are set up permanently and the rope can be clipped into the bolts that are already in place. On a natural crag the climber has to place his own protection. Some people find they can climb to quite a high technical difficulty indoors then, when they go outdoors, they haven't got some of the skills required to climb quite safely. Those skills take time and judgement to develop. Having said that, there are walls where you can place natural protection and there are courses that help people get the skills needed to go away and try to perfect the craft.

And, finally, Stanage is so popular because it is accessible. It can be reached very quickly from Sheffield, Manchester, Chesterfield, South Yorkshire and there's plenty of parking. If they go to Scotland, the Lake District or Wales climbers have to carry their gear a lot further. Climbers are lazy. People drive down from Edinburgh to Stanage for a weekend climb!

Being in the Mountain Rescue Team is not for the faint hearted. What makes them join? What makes them think 'I want to do that?

Most team members are active, hill-going people and see mountain rescue as an addition, an extension to what they already do. Some join because they've seen the work the team does or maybe because they've been to an accident or been involved in one. It's a sort of insurance policy because one day they might need it themselves.

Wanting to join the Mountain Rescue Team is only the beginning of a lengthy process. The applicant would be expected to navigate to a certain level. An interview day gives both existing team members and the person wanting to join the team an opportunity to see whether they would be able to fit into the structure of the service. There are some people who find they wouldn't be compatible with the commitment or the nature of how the

Wild flower meadow
© Robert Helliwell

Stanage
© Peak District National Park Authority

team operates.

That's the first stage followed by them being accepted as an 'Aspirant' when they will begin training that is wide ranging; working with helicopters, medical training, navigation, using ropes, radios and equipment. Mountain Rescue is a very specific activity and the training builds on the Aspirant's previous knowledge and skills to make them useful members of the team.

Team work is crucial. If you are going over the edge and somebody is holding your rope then you have to have a lot of trust in your team mates, your colleagues.

The training programme takes twelve to eighteen months to complete and by the time the trainee goes out on a rescue as a full team member they would be very unlikely to panic. If they did, the training would have failed.

A panic is one thing, a mild 'flap' another. That's part of the adrenalin rush of what they see and what is happening. Team work means there is always someone who is very calm and controlled at their shoulder saying 'Get on and do that'. The system would eliminate anybody who was a problem because it is so rigid.

There are things that the Aspirant wouldn't normally see, that he might not see until he's completed the training. He wouldn't normally be exposed to a fatality whereas, as a full team member, that is part of the job. No one gets used to being at the sharp end of serious accidents where there are awful injuries and whilst team members may come across as calm they aren't inside. Everybody deals with it differently. Team members support each other and the Team Leader and Chairman of the Team see giving support to members after a difficult rescue as one of their prime roles. If they don't want it, if they just want to talk, then that's what happens. There are quite a few doctors in the team and people who are used to dealing with the aftermath of accidents and their support is available to everyone. It's the whole team work thing.

Calls for the Team to go into action come through the Police and a minimum of twelve people are needed for a rescue. Usually there will be between twelve and eighteen people going out, maybe more, depending on what type of rescue it is and what time the call-out comes through. The Edale team also has three fully qualified dog-handlers who will bring their own search-and-rescue dogs out when they are needed.

There are seven Mountain Rescue Teams in the Peak District and each team has specific areas that they are responsible for. The controller takes the call from the Police, decides which team is needed, whether it's one or two teams that will work jointly, and will then contact the team who will call their members out.

There's a mixture of reasons for call-outs. Often it is bad weather – some of the bigger searches, the more serious ones, are often in periods of poor visibility or winter weather. But they can be anything from an ankle fracture to someone just being unable to continue for whatever reason. There are a lot of calls when people are overdue. People tend to panic very early when somebody doesn't turn up and they quite often walk into a pub on the wrong side of the hill when the team is being deployed or early in the operation!

A climbing accident on Stanage has a search party to find out exactly where there are on the Edge, which is six kilometres long.

There's different levels of search. It could be known that they are on Stanage but not exactly where they are or the Team is given a location of where somebody says they are only to find they're not and it becomes a search.

Getting vehicles to the site can prove difficult. There's one point where there is access but it's pretty bumpy. It's not fast and it's certainly off-road! Normally the team doesn't need to get any closer than the car parks and it is impossible to respond if they are going up the hill with a four-wheel vehicle. It's quicker to walk. The road is generally close enough. It's usually only to get heavy equipment in rather than getting people out that vehicles would be taken up as close as possible to Stanage Edge.

One of the biggest problems is finding the space to park. Eighteen people arriving at Stanage on a busy Bank-Holiday Monday means eighteen cars to park. But once they are on the Crag there's no problem. If it's busy, that's just how it is. People don't get in the way. More often they offer help and sometimes the Team accept it gratefully.

There's certain misunderstandings about climbers, boulderers and all the other people who go to Stanage to practise their sports. Whenever there's an accident the Press ask 'Are there any lessons to be learnt? What had they been doing wrong? Were they doing something stupid?'

The answer is 'No, of course they weren't. They had an accident. All sports have accidents.' It's rare to see sports people who are ill-equipped and accidents do happen. Anyone can make a mistake or do something wrong. To a certain extent accidents are always the result of a judgement that someone has made and that's how they get their experience. Nobody wants to go out there and fall off or get smashed against a rock.

There's no doubt that Team Members have a passion for the service but that doesn't stop it being frustrating. Very frustrating at times. Like the third call-out in the day or the family's just arrived from Australia and everyone's just sat down to Sunday lunch. Half-way through Christmas dinner or seven o'clock on New Year's Eve are good ones. They're frustrating.

The only way to react is to say 'Oh, not again,' and go and get on with it. That's just how it is. It's that sort of commitment and what's involved in being part of a rescue team that is difficult to get across to new members. They don't realise until they join a very busy team that there could be two call-outs on a Saturday, one on a Sunday, a day off Monday and Training on Tuesday. When Team work takes up six out of seven nights in the week it's guaranteed there'll be a call-out on the one free evening! They could almost be pencilled in the diary: 'Free Space – call out,' and it will happen!

All Team members and support staff give their time free of charge but funding the service is always an issue. It costs a massive £20,000 a year to run the team, to keep it ticking over, in addition to the call-outs, training, maintenance of the equipment and all of the administration costs. All of that has to come from contributions because there is absolutely no government or central funding.

There are collecting boxes in cafes and pubs, team members tin-rattle outside supermarkets and people who use Stanage and the surrounding area will sometimes send cheques in. Not for any particular reason, they just do.

A fair proportion comes from people who've had accidents and various small organisations or businesses have adopted the service as their charity for the year. Last year just one organisation sent a cheque for fourteen-hundred pounds which was fantastic. To put it in perspective, that one cheque will keep the team going for nearly a month.

It is difficult to keep the team going financially but government funding would be a bad idea. They'd certainly be looking at targets and that would be bad.

The Team has over forty members that can be called upon and there are around two-hundred members in the Peak District as a whole. It's purely because it's a voluntary service that those people are there and give their time.

"It can be very rewarding, annoying, a pain, frustrating and inconvenient, but when someone says 'Thank you' it's well worth it."

James Thacker, Neil Roden and Trevor Lawton.

Members of the Edale Mountain Rescue Team. Between them they have forty-three years service with the Mountain Rescue Service.

It is natural for anyone who has always had a deep interest in the countryside to visit the Stanage area. Rick Jilling's interest began as a child and has continued over the years, not only on a personal basis but also in his professional life. As a Ranger with the Derbyshire Countryside Service Rick spends his time caring for and about the environment and taking pleasure from maintaining the countryside for future generations.

My family had always been interested in the countryside and the great outdoors and walking was a part of that interest. What was a casual, family pastime led to me realising that the countryside was something that I'd be keen to develop as a career and would give me the opportunity to put something back into it. I did various voluntary work, initially with the

Peak District National Park as a conservation volunteer, helping out on working parties, looking after footpaths, that sort of thing, and was invited to register for a training course as a volunteer ranger. One of the first tasks I did on that training was dry-stone walling at North Lees. I was brought up in Elton, in the Peak District, so there was plenty of countryside on my doorstep but when I was about seventeen or eighteen, for the first time, I had the freedom of borrowing my mum's car and I explored the Peak District a bit more widely. Following on from that I did a lot of work with the PDNP as a volunteer and became a volunteer ranger with them and have subsequently gone on to be a ranger with the County Council.

Stanage has always been a special place. On a fine day there's nowhere better than the gritstone edges to walk and see the fantastic views.

I'm not a particularly good climber. I've got one or two friends who climb and I've enjoyed the climbing that I've done but I've not got the equipment and I've not really led climbs. I've never really had the time to spend as much time as I'd like to doing it.

One incident that made an impact as far as my own climbing and protection were concerned happened when I trained to become a Volunteer Ranger with the Peak District National Park Authority. I was about twenty at that time and I went out with one of the rangers from the Peak Park. Part of his duties was to patrol around Stanage and make sure the area was all right. We stopped to watch a few rock-climbers climbing on the edge at Stanage. One chap was climbing an overhang and he didn't have a helmet on but they had put bolts or 'protection' into the rocks to stop them falling and bouncing down the rock face. When it came to it the weight and the jolt pulled the protection out of the crack in the rock. He fell probably twenty feet and landed on the ground and unfortunately he did have quite a nasty head injury. He was drifting in and out of consciousness. I ran back to try and get a stretcher. There's a road below Stanage with a toilet block and Mountain Rescue keep a stretcher there. I was crossing fairly rough terrain carrying half a stretcher – the stretcher is in two parts that connect together – and I was wanting to be as prompt as possible but not wanting to rush, fall over and injure myself. I've got a very strong memory of wanting to do whatever I could to hopefully get that person to medical attention, to deal with the first aid side of it and to get the stretcher to him. I can remember weighing up the scenario, how to get that assistance to that person as quickly as possible. There was an adrenaline rush. The whole episode has stuck with me. The indirect feeback was that the person was okay. A very vivid memory.

Why do people come to Stanage, apart from the obvious beauty of the area? It's probably a little bit more accessible than other gritstone edges in that there's the village of Hathersage nearby. The tea-shops, walking and outdoor shops make it a mixed day out. If you are going out walking and it's absolutely pouring down with rain there's the fall-back of a large village with lots of interests to explore.

Hathersage being on the train lines means that people, particularly from Sheffield and Manchester, can jump on the train and get to Hathersage and use that as a stepping-board to get to Stanage.

The motor car and the railways have had a huge impact on the area. Probably more recently the motor car has been seen to cause problems of congestion and erosion but there's also the Hope Valley Railway that brings people in to a number of points in the Valley and Hathersage and Grindleford are key points on the Hope Valley line.

There's always talk about how many people go to Stanage but I wouldn't like other people to be denied an opportunity to use it. What I would say about the gritstone edges is that there are always a lot of places, if you take the time to study the map, if you know your way around the Peak District. You can always find the solitude. You can always find the peace, the tranquillity. It's a matter of looking at the map and exploring the open countryside a bit more widely. A lot of people who visit Stanage will know it because of its accessibility. Other people will explore a bit deeper to find somewhere they can be on their own. There's somewhere for everybody. Stanage is one piece of the jigsaw and if you're after rock faces, fantastic views and solitude, you can find that elsewhere as well. You wouldn't have to travel too far either. There are quiet places around.

When you look at the number of walking and climbing shops there are and the prices of the goods it could be said that the sports are becoming elitist but maybe it's that the outdoors is actually becoming more trendy. As a kid you'd have a blue kagool and that was what you would wear if it was raining and you'd get hot and sweaty. Now I think people have more money to spend on outdoor equipment and they're keen that the gear looks good, it's trendy and it does a good job. It keeps you cool, it keeps you dry and people are happy to view walking as a pastime and also climbing as a pastime and invest the money in it.

You can still get the cheap gear. You don't have to have a lot of money in your pocket. You can get walking boots, not particularly good ones, but you can get them for thirty or forty pounds. You can still get a raincoat for under twenty pounds but people seem to be happy to pay £200 for a flash Gortex in lovely colours. If they can afford it and if it helps to keep the rural economy going, hopefully it can benefit the area.

If you look at villages like Hathersage the character has changed with the new influx of the outdoor shops and that sort of thing, but the changes have helped to make a vibrant community. To keep jobs all year round you need something to bring in the visitors all year round and you need something for the wet as well as the dry days.

In terms of the effects on the environment of large numbers of people congregating in a small area there can be problems: litter, soil and vegetation erosion and also problems of erosion on the rock face as well. I work and live closer to the Wirksworth area rather than Stanage but certainly the pressure that comes to countryside sites can be a problem. Even with something like rock-climbing you can find that some climbers and visitors, not all, but a minority, can cause serious problems leaving litter and causing damage to the rock face itself. Actually chipping out hand-holds in the rock. At Black Rocks we've had gloss paint poured down the rock faces. But the vast majority are okay. They take care of the places they visit.

A big concern is that wild flowers are becoming scarcer and nesting birds are being disturbed because of the numbers of visitors and that produces a dilemma. Do you sacrifice Stanage and the surrounding area in order to protect somewhere else or do you try to stop the ravages that are happening?

Because Stanage is so accessible it would be very hard to preclude people from it, or even to control the numbers of people visiting there. The one thing that could be controlled is parking and vehicular access. Things like that can be looked at very carefully. There are remedial works that can be done in terms of path and vegetation erosion and creating paths. If you look at design lines on the ground to try and keep people to one particular route, a maintained route, it costs money and it takes a lot of staff time so the money has to be there to invest to stop the erosion taking place.

Practically it would be really hard to stop people coming to somewhere as well known as Stanage. If you put up signs asking people not to go there I think you would struggle. Stanage is inbuilt in peoples' map of the countryside, the map of the Peak District, and I think it's become a honey-pot that people will flock back to. So it's a case of trying to work to educate people into being more environmentally friendly on site, to reduce the amount of litter, to look carefully at landscaping schemes and erosion control schemes on the ground.

I mentioned previously that there are less well-known areas that are open for people to walk and to climb in so if Stanage was closed would there be a lot of impact when a lot of those areas became more well known? The problems of erosion and disturbance rather than being concentrated in one particular spot, would be widespread. In terms of litter picking – if there's a well-known site that you can monitor and maintain it's possibly better than having to look at a huge, wider area.

People don't only visit Stanage to climb, walk or para-glide. For many people there is something almost spiritual about the place. It's a fantastic area. You feel revived from being up on the gritstone edges, much wider than just Stanage. Certainly the gristone edges are fantastic, it's a feeling of being on top of the world; it's a feeling of having a reasonable breeze, if not a strong wind, blowing in your face; it's an area where you can get fantastic views or it's an area where it can be damp and bleak. It's nature and countryside saying something to you. Whether it's bare and slightly eroded soils, the bare rock, the expanse of the heather or the expanse of the view, it is quite a raw environment. And yes, it does bring you directly face to face with nature. You take that away with you and when you need to feel revived you go back again.

Rick Jillings

There is a lot of talk about how farming has changed but it might come as a surprise to newcomers to the area, or people not involved in the farming life, that many changes have taken place within the short time-span of the working lives of present day farmers. Jane Marsden came from a farming family at Ringinglow and moved to Thorpe Farm a couple of years after her marriage to John. His family had farmed in the area for many generations; his ancestors would recognise the need to diversify. It could be said the wheel has turned full circle.

Years ago it was common for people to have other jobs as well as farming their land and caring for their stock. That's how it is now.

We are the only dairy farmers who have farmed for generations that are left in Hathersage. When I first went to Thorpe Farm we had thirty-five or forty dairy cows. Now we've got one-hundred-and-forty and we run accommodation as well.

Years ago we had a milk round too. My father-in-law used to do it but when he gave it up there was only my husband, myself and a lad working the farm – the 'lad' still works for us. I'd got three little boys and by the time I'd got them dressed, got the milk loaded up and went off to do the round it had become really hard work, so we sold it on.

We've only got one neighbour who still farms and before he retired he had a full-time job as well. We looked up John's grandfather in the census and he wasn't just a farmer; he was a carter too, so he had two incomes.

They had to scrat around.

Now we're looking at additional ways of earning our livings. There's the possibility of getting funding for a mobile processing plant to make our own cheese. We'd buy in the use of it for however many days a month we wanted it and we'd have storage facilities and hook-up points and so on at the farm. Then it would be possible to go to the Tourist Market with our product.

We're thinking about that one.

The Farmers Markets have sprung up everywhere and they're a good thing but you have to find the time to do all these things. The market ties up a whole day as well as packing the day before. If we were delivering to other outlets that would be another drain on our time. There are only so many hours in the day and if it starts to affect the core businesses it's not worth it. We can't really afford to be away from the farm because of the accommodation we offer. We've got to be there in case people turn up.

One way to manage it would be to network; if people had farm shops we could sell our own and other people's produce and they would do the same.

But, whichever way you look at it, it's a very different way of earning a living, isn't it?

Jane Marsden

As Land Agent Matthew Croney is professionally involved with Stanage and the North Lees Estate whilst as a mountain biker and walker he enjoys the area in his leisure time.

What is a Land Agent? Well, traditionally a Land Agent's work would be based on agriculture and traditional land management but on an estate like this it's far more wide-ranging and that's what interested me in the job. I tend to use the title Estate Manager as it's easier to understand. The Estate Manager is the central point, the co-ordinator, so I have to try and make all of the elements fit together; Stanage and North Lees is one of the most visited areas of the countryside in Britain; it's designated as a special protection area for wildlife, for its rare birds and is a special area for conservation for its habitats; it has a working farm that is run by Derby College, so education plays a big part; it has four scheduled monuments so archaeology is important and it has all types of recreation. Add on to that the local population of Hathersage, which is not too far away, and you begin to see the variety of my job.

There's never a dull day! At the moment my time is heavily involved in people management. I've come to regard them as part of the habitat. North Lees includes the people and the recreational activities that the people take part in.

One of my fundamental beliefs is that people have a natural affinity with nature or they are in favour of nature, are supportive, however latent that is, and it's just a case of promoting understanding about what nature there is at Stanage and what people can do to help. Ninety-nine percent of people, in my experience, will go along with what you ask them if you explain the wildlife benefits.

That's where the Stanage Forum has come into its own.

> **"During one very heavy snow fall in 1969 Oliver Archer came down to Thorpe Farm. He sat in my mother-in-law's kitchen and we couldn't get rid of him round the fire. Then we discovered that up at Upperhurst, where he farmed, the snow had come from a different direction and they couldn't open the door for the snow. He'd climbed out through the kitchen window and then the window wouldn't shut properly. He'd come down for a warm because it was so cold down there."**

Where did the Stanage Forum idea come from? The idea for a Forum started germinating in 1996 when I began the job of managing the Estate. The 'Pay and Display' machine had just gone into the main car park and other car parks were being built, along with earth mounding, to try to prevent roadside parking. There was a terrific adverse reaction to that. In the first year of operation the 'Pay and Display' machine was vandalised twelve times. Any sign of the Authority, including the interpretation board in the car park, went. The British Mountaineering Council mounted a campaign in the climbing magazines and stickers appeared in car windscreens; 'Say No To Tax On Access'.

Where things had gone wrong, I believe, was that no one had been consulted. As I understand it, the BMC was told what was happening just a week before the 'Pay and Display' machine went in so there was a lot of animosity. I felt it was mainly based on misunderstanding but it took a long time, probably two years, to get a really good working relationship with the BMC again. My bosses put out constant press releases, answered all the accusations and explained that it was a charge on a polluting form of transport and not a tax on access. We also tried to make clear the fact that it was a means of re-investing in the estate and public transport and that it wouldn't prevent people from coming onto the estate.

About that time the Local Agenda 21 idea was really taking off, bringing things down to a much more local level and involving people more in decisions that affected their lives. Tim Richardson, from Sheffield University, who had associations with the Park through his previous work, suggested a rough idea. Why not try something in line with Local Agenda 21 to try to resolve all these conflicts? The idea struck a chord with me straight away. It was an opportunity to manage Stanage, such an iconic place, with a much more enlightened approach, involving stakeholders in decisions. That started it really. I began by finding out more about the approach and the more I found, the more encouraged I became. From start to finish I felt that it was the right thing to do. I wrote to everybody I could think of, asking if they thought it was a good idea and they over-whelmingly said yes. The Countryside Agency part-funded it, as a national pilot project, and the Peak District National Park Authority and the British Mountaineering Council also put money into it. Everybody was in favour of this approach although there was some concern at the National Park about how I would find the time to do it. To my mind, the single most important thing for my job was a management plan for the estate. You can't manage an estate effectively without a plan and all these issues needed resolving and would have taken an enormous amount of my time anyway, so why not do it in this way?

We appointed a consultant as facilitator because we felt we needed somebody who was completely independent, because of the conflicts, and we didn't feel we were sufficiently experienced in this particular approach. He advised us to form a steering group and to get people involved straight away in designing the process, before we put any concrete ideas down on paper. We had to start somewhere so we got ten people, from a range of different interests, together and most of them went on to be members of the Steering Group. They roughed out a time scale and possible structure, which ended up being the structure we agreed at the first big Forum event. There were four public meetings, everyone who was interested could attend, and we had a web site with a discussion board and news letters.

The Steering Group dealt with all of the detail and co-ordinated the process. We had to be very upfront from the beginning that the Peak District National Park Authority had the right to make final decisions but we never actually exercised it. There was no need. Officers were involved at every stage and we had consensus as a founding principle. I was in a good position personally because I use the area for recreation as well as managing the Estate. I'm a mountain biker and walker, that's how I first became interested in rural issues and developed my passion for nature conservation, so I genuinely have got that middle view. I have got that balance of recreation and conservation. I think the people on the Steering Group recognised that and appreciated it.

Why do so many people visit Stanage and the North Lees Estate? When the Forum first started we asked people 'What do you most value about the area?' We personalised it. The top answers were the nature, beauty, landscape, wild life, all of those sorts of things. So they visit the area to climb or walk but more specifically to climb and walk in that environment.

We can't ignore that Stanage is such an icon to climbers and walkers. People started climbing here back in the 1890's and it was one of the first open access areas in the National Park. Sheffield became a real cultural centre for climbing long ago and it's the first Edge that people coming out of Sheffield can see. They come out of the city, up on to the moorland edge, over the top and there's Stanage. It must have such a dramatic impact on people.

The Hope Valley is also such a tourist corridor and Stanage is one of the first places tourists come to in the Valley. It's the start of a number of circular walks, too.

There are other attractions as well. Broomfield (now Derby) College came in the late 80's, so the agricultural profile was raised then. The demonstration Hill Farm for Derbyshire; that's what it was seen as when they took over the tenancy. At one time the Hall was the most important feature of the Estate. The building is beautiful and people visit for the literary associations with Charlotte Bronte as well. Now the emphasis has changed. It's very much on The Edge now.

The Estate has an effect on the local economy; it's had a particularly beneficial effect on Hathersage in terms of providing customers. But tourism has changed the character of the village, which many people would say is not for the better. Many of the old grocers and butchers shops, the local shops for local people, have been replaced by outdoor clothing and equipment shops, but they might have gone anyway and the local shops that are left are benefiting from more people being there, more tourists coming in. They probably couldn't survive on just the local population now.

It depends on who you ask but many of the old inhabitants would say that it's reduced the quality of village life. But there's a lot more diversity now. There are people from all over the country coming in and they bring a certain view of the world with them that can enrich a community. But ninety-five percent of the people who come to Stanage come by car and that has largely destroyed the old way of life. I'd say that is the single thing that's changed things for the worse in the whole area.

What do I hope for the future? More of what we're achieving now. Five years ago the footpath across the middle of the bog on the top of the Edge was about twenty feet wide in places where people had gone around wet areas. We put signs either end explaining that it is an important moorland with important birds breeding there. We asked them to avoid the very wet shortcut and to use the alternative route that is slightly longer but more robust. Ninety-five percent of people do that and it's regenerated incredibly, you virtually can't see the path. I'd like to see us building on the greater understanding that we've got and on the working relationships that are already there. The Ring Ouzel issue is an example. One of the first really big things we rolled out from the new Management Plan was protecting these rare birds. Ring Ouzels are now Red Listed so they are a major conservation concern. Their population has declined more than fifty percent in the last ten years and Stanage seems to be one of the last southerly strongholds for them. But they like to nest on the crag, or at the base of it, on probably the busiest crag in the world, certainly the busiest in the UK, so to protect them is difficult. But we managed to get agreement. We had two successful nests right in the middle of the 'Popular End' of Stanage, right on the crag. People avoided those areas for the crucial four-week period from building a nest to chicks fledgling. The BMC, the hang-gliders and para-gliders have been fantastic in their support for that and it's been an unbelievable success.

> **"Old School House when it was for sale. The people who wanted it didn't have very much money. He came from farming stock and she was the daughter of a clergyman. They were such delightful people that I prayed and hoped that they might be able to buy it."**

All the people who use the area care passionately about it. We want to continue to involve them and harness that passion so that they feel a sense of collective responsibility and ownership. They are starting to report back to us, to tell us about things they've seen. They are starting to let us know about the birds. We've chosen the Ring Ouzel as an indicator, a key species for the Estate because it is right on the balance between recreation, agriculture and conservation. People are starting to ring in and tell us where they've seen Ring Ouzels nesting. That's really encouraging. I like that because it shows that people are taking an interest and an 'ownership' of these amazing birds. Some of the bird people get a bit worried about it because they can't put hearsay into a scientific report but the answer is that at least they are telling us. We can then investigate and report back on it.

How are other birds faring on such a busy estate? We've had various surveys done on birds since 1998 onwards and there generally seems to be a lot more of them about now. A lot of it is the result of tireless work by Bill Gordon and Flo Richardson, the Estate Wardens, in the woodlands, behind the scenes, developing the undergrowth, creating brash piles, widening fences around plantations to allow them to 'breathe', removing conifers, fencing the sheep out. This work takes a long time to come to fruition but we're now seeing the benefits. The woodlands are alive with birds now. It's fantastic. But a few years ago bird populations were at a low ebb on the Estate, mainly because people were parking everywhere around the moorland and walking straight from their cars to the Edge through previously quiet areas. There was also a problem with overgrazing by the sheep.

When I started my job we didn't, to my knowledge, have any reed bunting or linnet. Now we've got them both and snipe, curlew and whinchat have returned to their former levels too. Asking people to keep to the main paths and not cut across the moorland is paying off.

As individual contributors, Bill and Gordon and Flo Richardson have had a tremendous impact on the estate in a very subtle way. They've been a great inspiration to me; their total dedication to the cause, to the National Park's fundamental purposes and just the way they go about their work. They are very deep thinkers and the work that they do is with a very light touch but very effective. And they're always learning, that's the great thing. They could say 'I'm in my fifties now, I've been doing this job for twenty years, there's nothing I don't know about managing the Estate'. Most people in that position would do and just carry on doing what they've always done but not Bill and Flo - they are always constantly learning, changing and developing.

My real wish for the future, and the really big issue that we've got to tackle, is traffic and parking. To get people to leave their cars at home or to avoid coming when they know it is busy. Just to reduce the numbers of cars to an acceptable level so that we can maintain that wild feel to the area. That's it. It's a whole shift of culture. It's a problem we face as a nation. It's not going to be easy. It will need a lot of persistence and co-ordinated effort and joint promotion. Will it happen? I don't know, but then, you never know with Stanage what's going to happen next. As I said before, there's never a dull day.

Matthew Croney

USEFUL INFORMATION

British Mountaineering Council: www.bmc.co.uk
Matthew Croney – Estate Manager for North Lees Estate
        e-mail: mc@peakdistrict-npa.gov.uk
Derbyshire Cave Rescue: www.hnh.dircon.co.uk/dcro
Guide Dogs for the Blind: www.guidedogs.org.uk
Local Studies Library, Cultural & Community Services, Matlock. 01629 580000
National Search and Rescue Dog Association: www.nsarda.org.uk
Peak District National Park Authority: 01629 816200
The Ramblers Association: www.ramblers.org.uk
Sheffield Group of the Ramblers Association: Information from
sheffield.rambers@care4free.net or Jack Burling: 0114 230 1015
Stanage Forum: www.peakdistrict.org (Click on the Stanage Forum link
        under 'Working Together')
Tourist Information Centres: Buxton 01298 25106
                            Bakewell 01629 813227

Climbing Walls:
Heeley Millennium Boulder, Heeley Park, Sheffield
Matrix Bouldering Arena, Sheffield. 0114 222 6950 www.usport.co.uk
Ponderosa Boulder, off Crookes Valley Road, Sheffield
The Edge Climbing Centre, Sheffield. 0114 275 8899 www.sheffield-climbing.com
The Foundry, Sheffield: 0114 279 6331 www.foundryclimbing.com
Wirksworth Climbing Wall, Derbyshire 01629 824717
        www.derbyshiredales.gov.uk

Edale Mountain Rescue: www.edalemrt.co.uk
In an emergency:
Go to the nearest phone
Dial 999
Ask for Police and Mountain Rescue
Give: exact location of incident and nature of injuries
the number of casualties
your phone number
'ay near the phone unless instructed otherwise